American Homestead
Christmas

21 Felt & Fabric Projects for Homemade Holidays

Ellen Murphy

C&T PUBLISHING

Text copyright © 2015 by Ellen Murphy

Photography and artwork copyright © 2015 by C&T Publishing, Inc.

Publisher: Amy Marson

Creative Director: Gailen Runge

Art Director: Kristy Zacharias

Editor: Lynn Koolish

Technical Editors: Ellen Pahl and Amanda Siegfried

Cover Designer: April Mostek

Book Designer: Christina Jarumay Fox

Production Coordinators: Zinnia Heinzmann and Jenny Davis

Production Editor: Alice Mace Nakanishi

Illustrator: Tim Manibusan

Photo Assistant: Mary Peyton Peppo

Style photography by Nissa Brehmer and instructional photography by Diane Pedersen, unless otherwise noted

Published by C&T Publishing, Inc., P.O. Box 1456, Lafayette, CA 94549

All rights reserved. No part of this work covered by the copyright hereon may be used in any form or reproduced by any means—graphic, electronic, or mechanical, including photocopying, recording, taping, or information storage and retrieval systems—without written permission from the publisher. The copyrights on individual artworks are retained by the artists as noted in *American Homestead Christmas*. These designs may be used to make items for personal use only and may not be used for the purpose of personal profit. Items created to benefit nonprofit groups, or that will be publicly displayed, must be conspicuously labeled with the following credit: Designs copyright © 2015 by Ellen Murphy from the book *American Homestead Christmas* from C&T Publishing, Inc. Permission for all other purposes must be requested in writing from C&T Publishing, Inc.

Attention Copy Shops: Please note the following exception—publisher and author give permission to photocopy pages 56–78 for personal use only.

Attention Teachers: C&T Publishing, Inc., encourages you to use this book as a text for teaching. Contact us at 800-284-1114 or ctpub.com for lesson plans and information about the C&T Creative Troupe.

We take great care to ensure that the information included in our products is accurate and presented in good faith, but no warranty is provided nor are results guaranteed. Having no control over the choices of materials or procedures used, neither the author nor C&T Publishing, Inc., shall have any liability to any person or entity with respect to any loss or damage caused directly or indirectly by the information contained in this book. For your convenience, we post an up-to-date listing of corrections on our website (ctpub.com). If a correction is not already noted, please contact our customer service department at ctinfo@ctpub.com or at P.O. Box 1456, Lafayette, CA 94549.

Trademark (™) and registered trademark (®) names are used throughout this book. Rather than use the symbols with every occurrence of a trademark or registered trademark name, we are using the names only in the editorial fashion and to the benefit of the owner, with no intention of infringement.

Library of Congress Cataloging-in-Publication Data

Murphy, Ellen, 1960-

American Homestead Christmas : 21 felt & fabric projects for homemade holidays / Ellen Murphy.

pages cm

ISBN 978-1-61745-049-5 (soft cover)

1. Christmas decorations. 2. Textile crafts. I. Title.

TT900.C4M86 2015

745.594'12--dc23

2014047454

Printed in China

10 9 8 7 6 5 4 3 2 1

DEDICATION

For those who share my American homestead:
Robert, Katie Rose, Brennan,
and Mia the Wonder Dog.

ACKNOWLEDGMENTS

Many thanks to my family for all the Christmas memories we have created through the years.

Thank you to my friends who share their thoughts on my projects, laugh with me at our Me Time sessions, and always share their Christmas cookie recipes.

Thank you to the wonderful world for the endless inspiration— the work of artisans, ancient and contemporary, influences me every day.

Thanks to National Nonwovens and Timeless Treasures Fabrics for their contributions to this book.

Thanks to C&T Publishing: Amy and Gailen—it was so much fun to talk about ideas at Quilt Market (I still think the ornaments would look great as sugar cookies); Roxane, from whom I learn so much about the industry in our always-informative talks; Lynn, who answers all my questions; Ellen, who makes sure that what I write about my designs is correct; April, for the lovely cover; Christina, who makes everything look so beautiful; and everyone else at C&T Publishing who contributed to this book.

And special thanks to the residents of my American homestead, Avalon. To Robert, my Mr. Wonderful; my children, Katie Rose and Brennan; and Mia the Wonder Dog.

Contents

Introduction

Christmas is a magical and enchanting time of year. It's when we have a chance to celebrate with friends and family and catch up with people far and wide through Christmas cards. We relive special times from the past by telling the younger members of the family stories from the old days, and we have the opportunity to start new traditions.

I grew up in a small town just outside New York City, so I was lucky to be able to experience both an old-fashioned quiet town and the bright lights of the big city. When I was young, my hometown had a thriving downtown filled with shops and restaurants. The streets were festooned with lights and holiday decor, and the shops would stay open late so people could shop after work. For us kids, it was so fun to see the town decorated and often covered in snow. The sidewalks were bustling with people, and you could stop to chat with friends and neighbors. It all added to the excitement of the season.

At home we baked cookies with our mom. I especially loved the Swedish spritz cookies made with the Mirro cookie press; we loved to make all the different shapes and then decorate them with colored sugars and sprinkles. By Christmas day, we had Christmas from around the world on our dessert table—we would exchange baked goods with friends and family, and we got to sample the favorite recipes from so many cultures.

A short train or bus ride would take us to New York City. Manhattan during the holiday season is wonderful! Sidewalk vendors roast chestnuts, the windows in the big stores on Fifth Avenue are beautifully decorated, the tree is up at Rockefeller Center, and we can watch the skaters below. The highlight of the Christmas season in New York is the Christmas show at Radio City. Back in those days, Radio City was a movie theater with a stage show. You bought a ticket to enter, and I suppose you could have stayed all day if you wanted. We would time it so we could watch the stage show, see the movie, and then watch the stage show again. My favorite part was the "living Nativity" with all the live animals—camels, donkeys, and sheep. The huge stage of Radio City was filled with people and animals, and even along the side there were little areas filled with more people and animals. The song "O Holy Night" was my favorite, when it got to the part with …

Fall on your knees,
O hear the angel voices,
O night divine!

… the entire cast would fall to their knees (and in my memory the animals would too, but I can't confirm that). Just thinking of it can still bring tears to my eyes.

We were lucky in my family because most of my cousins and aunts and uncles lived in the same small town. We grew up with family parties at all the holidays. As time went by, things began to change. My brother, for example, hosted an annual Christmas Eve family open house. As a fundraiser, our town began selling luminaria kits, and on Christmas Eve almost everyone in town lined the edges of their property with the luminaria. It was stunning.

Then I grew up and it was time to start my own family traditions. For me, Christmas is centered on the home. In our house, the decorations come out after Thanksgiving. The cards start arriving, and we hang them in swags around the house. We pore over cookie recipes and begin our baking.

I think we should experience the joy of Christmas every day, and I work on projects and presents all year long. With all the chaos in our fast-paced world, I enjoy working on stitching projects throughout the year. I like that I have to slow down and enjoy what I am doing.

Much of the inspiration for my designs comes from folk traditions I have discovered in my travels around the world. While most tourists are visiting the grand museums, you'll find me at the local folk art museum or a museum of ethnography. I also roam through the local markets, checking out handcrafts from the region. I'm always amazed at the beauty of folk art creations that are made with humble materials and lots of imagination.

I hope you enjoy the projects in this book as much as I have. Start making or adding to the Christmas memories of your family. Teach a child to embroider! Make little handmade gifts for all your children or grandchildren so they can then take them on to their households in the future; your gifts will become treasured heirlooms.

I want to thank all the people who have added to my Christmas memories—you have all made my world brighter. Peace on Earth.

From my American homestead to wherever you may call home.

All the best,
Ellen

Using Felt

I've been saying, "Felt is the new black" for a while now. I think wool felt has become popular because it has come such a long way from the ten-for-a-dollar felt pieces we used to buy. Now many of the felts are very high quality, and you can find them in fabulous colors.

I like to work in wool felt because I like the crispness of the edges and the way the embroidery stitches show up so nicely on it. This does not mean that the felt projects can only be made in wool felt; felted woven wool works just as well, if that's what you prefer.

COLOR OPTIONS

All the projects in this book are made in what I call my European Folk Art Collection of colors. I realize many people prefer other color schemes and have different styles of decorating in their homes, so I have included multiple colorways for the nine felt ornament projects. There are examples of a darker group of colors that I call my Pennyrug Collection, and also the Traditional Christmas Collection, which has red, greens, gold, and white. Of course, you can create your own favorite color schemes using any colors you prefer. Note that the colors shown here are available from National Nonwovens (see Resources, page 79).

Ornament made from felted woven wool

EUROPEAN FOLK ART COLLECTION	
Barnyard Red	
Pea Soup	
Fresh Linen	
Tropical Wave	
Butternut Squash	

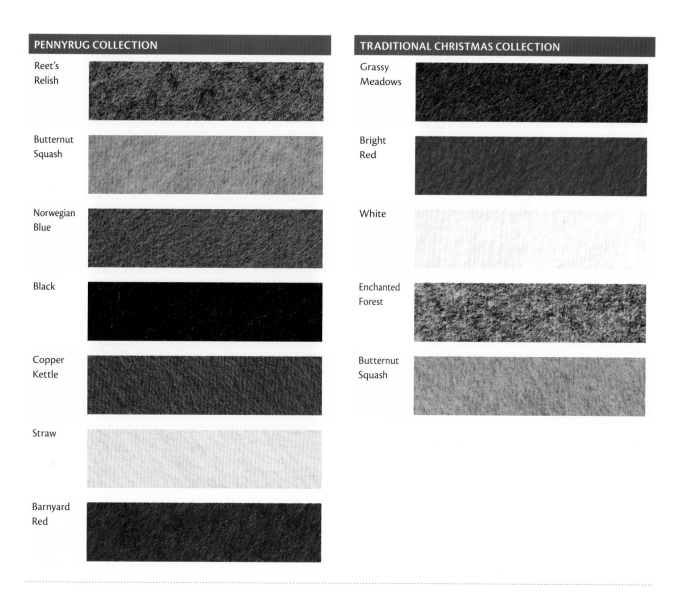

PENNYRUG COLLECTION		TRADITIONAL CHRISTMAS COLLECTION	
Reet's Relish		Grassy Meadows	
Butternut Squash		Bright Red	
Norwegian Blue		White	
Black		Enchanted Forest	
Copper Kettle		Butternut Squash	
Straw			
Barnyard Red			

You can also make the projects in other colors, for other seasons or holidays.

For example, make them for spring or fall in appropriate colors.

Spring colors

Fall colors

USING THE DESIGNS

You can use the felt designs in the book in a number of ways. The project instructions show you how to create the designs; you decide what to make with them.

■ As an ornament

Cut out 2 layers of quilt batting, reusing the freezer-paper template from the largest shape of the ornament; trim away ¼" from the edges. After you have finished the stitching and embroidery of the ornament, sandwich the batting between the appliquéd shape (the top) and the plain shape (the bottom). Use a whipstitch around the edge to finish. Add a loop of floss or narrow ribbon to the back for hanging.

■ As decor

Make the piece as you would for the pincushion or ornament—your choice depends on whether you want it to be full like the pincushion or flatter like the ornament. Cut a scrap of felt 2" × ⅞" and pin it to the back. Sew both sides and the top using a whipstitch; leave the bottom edge open. Slip a ¼" dowel rod into this sleeve and place the other end of the dowel rod into a 2½" × 2½" block of wood with a ¼" hole drilled into the center. Stain or paint the wood as desired.

■ As a pincushion

After you have finished the stitching and embroidery on the top of the felt, layer the shape over the plain shape of the same size. Whipstitch around the edges to close it, leaving a small opening for stuffing. Insert fiberfill until it is well stuffed and then finish stitching the opening closed.

■ In a frame

Cut a piece of felt 6" × 6", center a small ornament design on top of it, and sew together using a whipstitch around the edge of the ornament. Attach this square to a 6" × 6" square of foam core board using spray adhesive and place it in a needlework frame with a 6" × 6" opening.

Information for All Projects

MAKING TEMPLATES

My method of using the patterns in the book is to make templates by tracing the patterns onto the dull (or paper) side of freezer paper. If you are making just one of a felt project, you can trace the patterns from the book right onto the dull side of freezer paper.

If you are making multiple items from the same pattern, it's best to make cardboard or poster board templates that you can trace around. I use dressmaker's tracing/transfer sheets that I place between the original pattern and the cardboard or poster board. When you draw over the original pattern, it transfers to the board underneath. You can also use graphite or carbon paper in the same manner. Cut the cardboard shape out carefully along the transferred lines.

Each pattern indicates the quantity you need to trace and cut. Most of the patterns in the book are the exact shape and size needed, but some of the larger patterns will need to be traced onto folded freezer paper. These patterns have arrows along the edges that indicate where to place them on the folds of the freezer paper to make a complete freezer-paper template.

For complete patterns without arrows, trace the pattern from the book page (or the poster board shape) onto the dull (paper) side of the freezer paper. Trim the freezer paper about ¼" away from the outside of the drawn line.

For the patterns with arrows:

1. Make sure the piece of freezer paper is large enough for the complete pattern; then fold the freezer paper as indicated for the specific project.

2. Line up the arrows on the pattern along the folded edges of the freezer paper.

3. Trace along the edges that do not have arrows. I find it's easiest to put a few staples in the paper just outside the traced lines to hold it securely. This helps keep the pattern even and will make the shape more precise when you cut on the line.

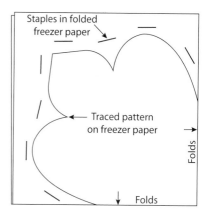

Add staples around traced lines.

4. Cut the freezer-paper template carefully along the drawn lines.

> ### tip
> With 8½″ × 11″ sheets of freezer paper, you can use a copier or inkjet printer to copy the patterns directly onto the freezer paper. Just be sure to feed the freezer paper into the printer or copier one sheet at a time and load the sheets so the printing will be on the dull side. You can buy precut sheets such as Quilter's Freezer Paper Sheets (by C&T Publishing).

USING THE TEMPLATES

To use a freezer-paper template, place it dull side up on the felt (so the shiny side touches the felt). Gently press with a medium-hot iron—you just want the template and felt to stick together but not fuse together.

I use sharp sewing scissors to cut large pieces and shorter scissors to cut small pieces; the ends are pointed and the blades are very sharp all the way to the point.

Carefully cut either along the traced lines of the shape (for templates that were cut ¼" outside the line) or along the edge of the template (for templates that were folded and cut on the drawn line). Gently remove the freezer paper. Your felt pieces are ready to use.

Always read the information on the patterns and refer to the instructions for each project.

■ For the ornaments, pincushions, and decor options, cut 2 of the largest shape for the item—either a circle or a square.

■ For the framed option or the *Nine-Patch Wallhanging* (page 41), cut 1 of the largest circle or square shape.

A NOTE ON THE SIZE OF THE ORNAMENTS

The ornaments are based on either a circle or a square. They come in two sizes: large and small. All ornaments use the same patterns for the background squares and circles (page 56). Additional patterns for each ornament will be found on a separate page, labeled with the name of the ornament.

The large sizes are perfect for the *Nine-Patch Wallhanging* (page 41). This is the size I use for ornaments for a large Christmas tree as well because they stand out (and you want them to stand out after all your hard work). The smaller size is used for the framed design and for smaller ornaments. If, however, you would like to make the ornaments even smaller for a mini tree or to use as pins or gift tags, you can reduce the size of the patterns on a home printer or copy machine. Just remember to reduce all the patterns for the specific ornament by the same percentage.

SEWING THE FELT DESIGNS

To appliqué the felt pieces to each other, use two strands of embroidery floss for all stitching and use either a whipstitch or blanket stitch. I use a short quilting needle to stitch, but try different types to find the one that is most comfortable and works best for you.

Pin the pieces together before stitching, inserting one or more pins as needed to prevent shifting. Remove the pins as you stitch.

EMBELLISHING

I use embroidery stitches to embellish the felt projects, but there are other options. If you like the look of beads, you could use them instead of the French knots, for instance.

Another idea would be to use decorative hot fix crystals. Be creative!

Try beading or decorative crystals.

EMBROIDERY STITCHES

Each project has specific instructions for stitching and embroidery—refer to the color photo or illustrations for the placement and color of embroidery stitches. Use two strands of embroidery floss for all stitches. For French knots, wrap the thread around the needle five times to make a nice chunky knot that shows up against the felt.

French knot. Make 5 wraps for a chunky knot.

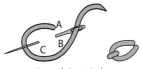

Lazy daisy stitch

Running stitch

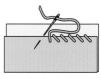

Blanket stitch

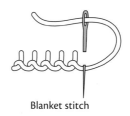

Whipstitch

PROJECTS

MERRY

FINISHED ORNAMENTS
Large: 4⅞" × 4⅞"
Small: 4⅛" × 4⅛"

CHRISTMAS MEMORIES Creativity Never Goes on Vacation

I'm sure I'm not the only creative person who needs a little vacation craft to take along on holidays. We need something to keep us busy on planes, trains, and car trips. This trip was a river cruise on the *Viking Sky*. We were cruising along the Danube River and visiting many of the Christmas markets between Budapest and Passau, Germany. I brought along some kits I had made up to make felt Christmas ornaments.

One day while we were cruising through the scenic Wachau Valley I took my stitching to the lounge. Soon enough, a lovely ten-year-old girl popped into the seat next to me and asked, "What's that?" I said, "It's embroidery. Do you want to learn how to do it?" And that was the beginning of a lovely friendship. Olivia and I would stitch on bus trips to distant cities and meet each night after dinner for our "stitching dates" in the lounge. We met just about everyone on the ship. People would stop by to chat and tell us stories about their moms and grandmas. When I got home I showed people the ornaments I had made and they loved them—that was the start of the American Homestead Folk Art Feltwork patterns.

MATERIALS

Refer to Color Options (page 6); for patterns, refer to Ornament Backgrounds (page 56) and Merry patterns (page 57).

COLORS AND QUANTITY OF WOOL FELT				
COLOR	LARGE ORNAMENT		SMALL ORNAMENT	
	Pattern	Amount needed	Pattern	Amount needed
Butternut Squash	1-A large	1 square 1½″ × 1½″	1-A small	1 square 1½″ × 1½″
Fresh Linen	1-B large	1 square 2″ × 2″	1-B small	1 square 2″ × 2″
Barnyard Red	1-C large	1 square 3″ × 3″	1-C small	1 square 3″ × 3″
Fresh Linen	1-D large	1 square 4″ × 4″	1-D small	1 square 3½″ × 3½″
Tropical Wave	1-E large	1 square 5″ × 5″	1-E small	1 square 4½″ × 4½″
Pea Soup	Large square	1 or 2 squares 5½″ × 5½″	Small square	1 or 2 squares 5″ × 5″

Other supplies:
- ■ Embroidery floss in assorted colors
- ■ Batting or fiberfill
- ■ Freezer paper

INSTRUCTIONS

Refer to Information for All Projects (page 9) for basic information on making and using templates and sewing.

1. Make the freezer-paper templates and cut the felt pieces.

2. Center circle 1-A on circle 1-B and sew together using a blanket stitch.

3. Center circle unit 1-A/B on flower shape 1-C and sew together along the edge of circle 1-B using a whipstitch. Make French knots inside the edge of circle 1-B.

4. Center cross shape 1-D on leaf shape 1-E and sew together using a whipstitch.

5. Center the 1-D/E unit on the felt background square and sew together along the edge of leaf shape 1-E using a whipstitch.

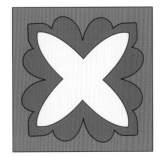

6. Center the 1-A/B/C unit on the 1-D/E/F unit and sew together along the edge of flower shape 1-C using a whipstitch. Make French knots along the inside edge of flower shape 1-C.

7. Use a lazy daisy stitch and French knots to make the designs in each of the 4 points of shape 1-D and in leaf shape 1-E as shown.

8. Refer to Using the Designs (page 8) for instructions and options to finish the project.

NOEL

FINISHED ORNAMENTS
Large: 4⅞" × 4⅞"
Small: 4⅛" × 4⅛"

CHRISTMAS MEMORIES The Great Tree Disaster of 1993

On the coldest day of 1993, Rob and I bundled up our fourteen-month-old daughter, Katie Rose, and four-month-old son, Brennan, and set off to a Christmas tree farm. We found a beautifully shaped tree, and Rob climbed under it to cut it down. We pulled it to the car, put the kids in their car seats, wrapped them in quilts, and spent the next hour battling a tree that was so frozen it would not bend. We couldn't get the thing on the roof of our car! The farmers finally came searching for us and found us scratched and shivering, with the unyielding tree still on the ground. They helped us get it secured to the roof, and off we headed for home, caroling all the way.

When we were setting the tree up in the house, it just did not want to stand up straight. The tree was next to our front windows, and I had the brilliant idea (I thought), to

wrap wire around the trunk and put an end of the wire through each of the windows and secure it to the brick post between the windows.

A few days later, Brennan was napping in his crib and Katie Rose had fallen asleep in my arms. I popped her in her playpen and went around the house trying to get some things done. I heard some little squeaking noises coming from the living room and thought, "Boy, that was a short nap!" When I walked into the living room, the tree was on its side covering the playpen. Katie Rose was peeking out below the branches. Once I was sure she was okay, I picked up that tree and threw it out on the front porch. We set it up outside under the front windows and there it stayed. We put a mini tabletop tree inside, and that was the last year we had a real tree.

MATERIALS

Refer to Color Options (page 6); for patterns, refer to Ornament Backgrounds (page 56) and Noel patterns (page 58).

COLORS AND QUANTITY OF WOOL FELT				
COLOR	LARGE ORNAMENT		SMALL ORNAMENT	
	Pattern	Amount needed	Pattern	Amount needed
Pea Soup	2-A large	1 square 1½″ × 1½″	2-A small	1 square 1½″ × 1½″
Barnyard Red	2-B large	1 square 2½″ × 2½″	2-B small	1 square 2¼″ × 2¼″
Butternut Squash	2-C large	1 square 2¾″ × 2¾″	2-C small	1 square 2½″ × 2½″
Fresh Linen	2-D large	1 square 4″ × 4″	2-D small	1 square 3½″ × 3½″
Pea Soup	2-E large	1 square 5″ × 5″	2-E small	1 square 4″ × 4″
Tropical Wave	Large square	1 or 2 squares 5½″ × 5½″	Small square	1 or 2 squares 5″ × 5″

Other supplies:
- Embroidery floss in assorted colors
- Batting or fiberfill
- Freezer paper

INSTRUCTIONS

Refer to Information for All Projects (page 9) for basic information on making and using templates and sewing.

1. Make the freezer-paper templates and cut the felt pieces.

2. Center circle 2-A on star shape 2-B and sew together using a whipstitch.

3. Center shape 2-C on shape 2-D as shown and sew together using a whipstitch.

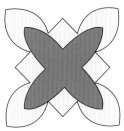

4. Center the 2-C/D unit on shape 2-E as shown and sew together along the edge of shape 2-D using a whipstitch.

5. Center the 2-A/B unit on the 2-C/D/E unit and sew together along the edge of shape 2-B using a whipstitch.

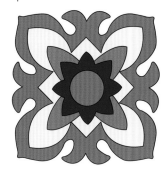

6. Center unit 2-A/B/C/D/E on the background and sew together along the edge of shape 2-E using a whipstitch.

7. Add decorative stitches as shown, using a lazy daisy stitch, running stitch, and French knots.

8. Refer to Using the Designs (page 8) for instructions and options to finish the project.

STARLIGHT

FINISHED ORNAMENTS
Large: 5" diameter
Small: 4¼" diameter

CHRISTMAS MEMORIES Christmas Surprise

In the years before our marriage, Rob and I lived in New Jersey near my family, but Rob's family lived twelve hours away in Michigan. One year, he wanted to go to Michigan, but we didn't want to miss sharing the holiday with my family, so we hatched a plan.

On Christmas Eve, we went to my brother's annual family open house, then to Midnight Mass, and then to my mom and dad's, where we opened presents. At about 4 a.m. we got in the car and headed west—we had carols on the radio, a cooler of food in the backseat, decorations in the back windows, and empty roadways.

We took turns driving (one of us slept while the other drove), and late that afternoon we pulled up to Aunt Peggy and Uncle Lou's house, where the whole Michigan gang was having Christmas dinner. We had on long overcoats, hats, and scarves, and I made songbooks out of paper to cover our faces. We rang the bell and stood in the middle of the lawn singing Christmas carols. It was just Aunt Peggy who came to the door, but we motioned to have the others come. A few people gathered at the door, including Rob's mom. Rob's sister Pat said, "Funny, that looks like Elle and Robert," and with that we showed our faces. Everyone screamed with delight. Of course, the others came running to see what was going on. Rob's mom said it was her best present!

MATERIALS

Refer to Color Options (page 6); for patterns, refer to Ornament Backgrounds (page 56) and Starlight patterns (page 59).

COLORS AND QUANTITY OF WOOL FELT				
COLOR	LARGE ORNAMENT		SMALL ORNAMENT	
	Pattern	Amount needed	Pattern	Amount needed
Fresh Linen	3-A large	1 square 1¼″ × 1¼″	3-A small	1 square 1¼″ × 1¼″
Butternut Squash	3-B large	1 square 2″ × 2″	3-B small	1 square 1¾″ × 1¾″
Tropical Wave	3-C large	1 square 3½″ × 3½″	3-C small	1 square 3″ × 3″
Pea Soup	3-D large	1 square 4½″ × 4½″	3-D small	1 square 4″ × 4″
Barnyard Red	3-E large	1 square 5″ × 5″	3-E small	1 square 4½″ × 4½″
Fresh Linen	Large circle	1 or 2 squares 5½″ × 5½″	Small circle	1 or 2 squares 5″ × 5″

Other supplies:

- Embroidery floss in assorted colors
- Batting or fiberfill
- Freezer paper

INSTRUCTIONS

Refer to Information for All Projects (page 9) for basic information on making and using templates and sewing.

1. Make the freezer-paper templates and cut the felt pieces.

2. Center circle 3-A on circle 3-B and sew together using a whipstitch.

3. Center circle unit 3-A/B on flower shape 3-C and sew together along the edge of circle 3-B using a whipstitch. Sew decorative stitches on the circles as shown, using a lazy daisy stitch and French knots.

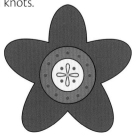

4. Center flower shape 3-E on the background circle and sew together using a whipstitch.

5. Place star shape 3-D on the background unit as shown and sew together along the edge of shape 3-D using a whipstitch.

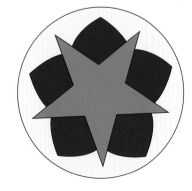

6. Center the 3-A/B/C unit on the background unit and sew together along the edge of shape 3-C using a whipstitch.

7. Sew decorative stitches on shapes 3-C, 3-D, and 3-E as shown, using a lazy daisy stitch, running stitch, and French knots.

8. Refer to Using the Designs (page 8) for instructions and options to finish the project.

HOLLY

FINISHED ORNAMENTS
Large: 4⅞" × 4⅞"
Small: 4⅛" × 4⅛"

CHRISTMAS MEMORIES My First Gift from Mr. Wonderful—an Ornament

Rob and I began dating in December 1982, while we were in college. His family lived in Michigan and he was going home for a month for the winter break. Before he left, I invited him and his roommate to come over to visit with my roommate and me. My roommate knew Rob, and I knew his roommate, so it was a pleasant evening of hanging out, eating treats, and watching Rob's roommate, Larry, do impersonations. Rob gave me my first present from him—a Christmas ornament, a little penguin named Perky. I never put this ornament away; it hangs on the wall in my quilt studio, and Mr. Wonderful and I are still happily celebrating Christmas together.

MATERIALS

Refer to Color Options (page 6); for patterns, refer to Ornament Backgrounds (page 56) and Holly patterns (page 60).

COLORS AND QUANTITY OF WOOL FELT				
COLOR	LARGE ORNAMENT		SMALL ORNAMENT	
	Pattern	Amount needed	Pattern	Amount needed
Barnyard Red	4-A large	1 square 2″ × 2″	4-A small	1 square 1¾″ × 1¾″
Pea Soup	4-B large	1 square 3″ × 3″	4-B small	1 square 2½″ × 2½″
Tropical Wave	4-C large	1 square 4″ × 4″	4-C small	1 square 3½″ × 3½″
Fresh Linen	4-D large	1 square 4″ × 4″	4-D small	1 square 3½″ × 3½″
Barnyard Red	Large square	1 or 2 squares 5½″ × 5½″	Small square	1 or 2 squares 5″ × 5″

Other supplies:
- Embroidery floss in assorted colors
- Batting or fiberfill
- Freezer paper

INSTRUCTIONS

Refer to Information for All Projects (page 9) for basic information on making and using templates and sewing.

1. Make the freezer-paper templates and cut the felt pieces.

2. Center shape 4-D on the background square and sew together using a whipstitch.

3. Center shape 4-C on the background unit and sew together along the edge of shape 4-C using a whipstitch.

4. Center shape 4-B on the background unit and sew together along the edge of shape 4-B using a whipstitch.

5. Center circle 4-A on the background unit and sew together along the edge of circle 4-A using a whipstitch.

6. Sew decorative stitches in the circle using running stitches and French knots.

7. Sew decorative stitches in shapes 4-B, 4-C, and 4-D as shown, using a lazy daisy stitch and French knots.

8. Refer to Using the Designs (page 8) for instructions and options to finish the project.

GLITTER

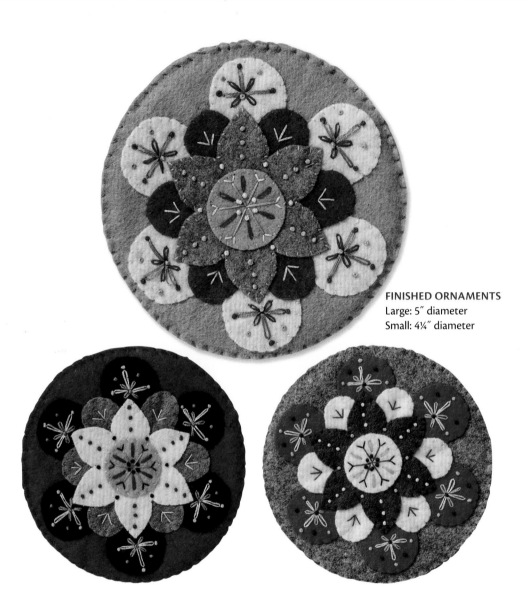

FINISHED ORNAMENTS
Large: 5″ diameter
Small: 4¼″ diameter

CHRISTMAS MEMORIES A Trunk Full of Traditions

Rob and I love antiques, and even before we were married we started buying treasures that would someday furnish our dream house. Of course, we were young and didn't have a lot of money, so we shopped at garage sales, church sales, and flea markets. At one garage sale we met a couple who were downsizing and selling an antique trunk filled with their 40-year collection of Christmas ornaments… all for $6. Of course we bought it, and we promised the couple we would take good care of the ornaments. We still use them on our family room tree and think of that couple every year.

MATERIALS

Refer to Color Options (page 6); for patterns, refer to Ornament Backgrounds (page 56) and Glitter patterns (page 61).

COLORS AND QUANTITY OF WOOL FELT				
	LARGE ORNAMENT		SMALL ORNAMENT	
COLOR	Pattern	Amount needed	Pattern	Amount needed
Butternut Squash	5-A large	1 square 2″ × 2″	5-A small	1 square 1¾″ × 1¾″
Tropical Wave	5-B large	1 square 3½″ × 3½″	5-B small	1 square 3″ × 3″
Barnyard Red	5-C large	1 square 4″ × 4″	5-C small	1 square 3½″ × 3½″
Fresh Linen	5-D large	1 square 5″ × 5″	5-D small	1 square 4½″ × 4½″
Pea Soup	Large circle	1 or 2 squares 5½″ × 5½″	Small circle	1 or 2 squares 5″ × 5″

Other supplies:
- Embroidery floss in assorted colors
- Batting or fiberfill
- Freezer paper

INSTRUCTIONS

Refer to Information for All Projects (page 9) for basic information on making and using templates and sewing.

1. Make the freezer-paper templates and cut the felt pieces.

2. Center circle 5-A on flower shape 5-B and sew together using a whipstitch.

3. Center flower shape 5-D on the background circle and sew together using a whipstitch.

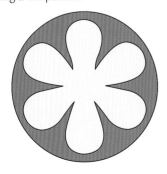

4. Center flower shape 5-C on the background unit and sew together along the edge of flower shape 5-C using a whipstitch.

5. Center the 5-A/B unit on the background unit and sew together along the edge of flower shape 5-B using a whipstitch.

6. Sew decorative stitches in the center circle as shown, using a running stitch, lazy daisy stitch, and French knots.

7. Sew decorative stitches in shapes 5-B, 5-C, and 5-D as shown, using a running stitch, lazy daisy stitch, and French knots.

8. Refer to Using the Designs (page 8) for instructions and options to finish the project.

JOLLY

FINISHED ORNAMENTS
Large: 4⅞" × 4⅞"
Small: 4⅛" × 4⅛"

CHRISTMAS MEMORIES Baking with Nut Cake

Years ago when I worked at an advertising agency, I had a coworker named Melissa. From talking at work we discovered we were kindred spirits: we loved crafts, we loved garage sales, we loved baking.

We decided to have a baking day to prepare for Christmas. Her house had a sunny enclosed porch, and we spent the day rolling out sugar cookies and gingerbread cookies on her grandmother's blue and white enamel-topped table. We were both artists, so we decorated the cookies beautifully. All the while, her cat, Nut Cake (Cakies, for short), was perched on one of the windowsills watching our every move. When we would finish a tray, we would put it on the dining room table so the icing could dry.

The next day Melissa called to say that some of the cookies had been given a bit of extra decoration. Sometime in the night, Cakies had pulled her claws through the icing of some of the cookies. I guess she just wanted to join in the baking fun!

MATERIALS

Refer to Color Options (page 6); for patterns, refer to Ornament Backgrounds (page 56) and Jolly patterns (page 62).

COLORS AND QUANTITY OF WOOL FELT				
COLOR	LARGE ORNAMENT		SMALL ORNAMENT	
	Pattern	*Amount needed*	*Pattern*	*Amount needed*
Butternut Squash	6-A large	1 square 1½″ × 1½″	6-A small	1 square 1½″ × 1½″
Tropical Wave	6-B large	1 square 2″ × 2″	6-B small	1 square 1¾″ × 1¾″
Fresh Linen	6-C large	4 squares 1½″ × 1½″	6-C small	4 squares 1½″ × 1½″
Fresh Linen	6-D large	1 square 3″ × 3″	6-D small	1 square 2½″ × 2½″
Barnyard Red	6-E large	1 square 4½″ × 4½″	6-E small	1 square 4″ × 4″
Pea Soup	Large square	1 or 2 squares 5½″ × 5½″	Small square	1 or 2 squares 5″ × 5″

Other supplies:

- Embroidery floss in assorted colors
- Batting or fiberfill
- Freezer paper

INSTRUCTIONS

Refer to Information for All Projects (page 9) for basic information on making and using templates and sewing.

1. Make the freezer-paper templates and cut the felt pieces.

2. Center circle 6-A on circle 6-B and sew together using a whipstitch.

3. Center shape 6-E on the background square and sew together using a whipstitch.

4. Center shape 6-D on the background unit as shown and sew together along the edge of shape 6-D using a whipstitch.

5. Center circle unit 6-A/B on the background unit and sew together along the edge of circle 6-B using a whipstitch.

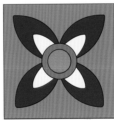

6. Place the heart shapes 6-C on the background between the leaf shapes 6-E as shown and sew together using a whipstitch.

7. Sew decorative stitches on the circle shapes using a lazy daisy stitch, running stitch, and French knots.

8. Sew decorative stitches on shapes 6-D, 6-E, and the background square using a running stitch and French knots.

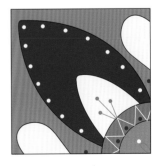

9. Refer to Using the Designs (page 8) for instructions and options to finish the project.

JOY

FINISHED ORNAMENTS
Large: 5″ diameter
Small: 4¼″ diameter

CHRISTMAS MEMORIES Lots of Ornaments, Lots of Fun

Because I am a collector and a crafter, our family has a lot of ornaments—too many for one tree. So the solution to that problem is to have more trees. In the front window of our living room we have a tree with white lights, white and crystal ornaments, garlands that look like icicles, clear beads, and antique prisms from old chandeliers that reflect the light beautifully. Our family room tree has the antique ornaments, ornaments from our travels, and homemade creations. When the kids were young, they each had a small tabletop tree in their bedroom where we would hang antique blocks and little toys. Just this year I bought a turquoise tree for my studio, and the European Folk Art felt ornaments look great on it!

MATERIALS

Refer to Color Options (page 6); for patterns, refer to Ornament Backgrounds (page 56) and Joy patterns (page 63).

COLORS AND QUANTITY OF WOOL FELT				
COLOR	LARGE ORNAMENT		SMALL ORNAMENT	
	Pattern	Amount needed	Pattern	Amount needed
Barnyard Red	7-A large	1 square 2″ × 2″	7-A small	1 square 1¾″ × 1¾″
Fresh Linen	7-B large	1 square 3″ × 3″	7-B small	1 square 2½″ × 2½″
Tropical Wave	7-C large	1 square 5¼″ × 5¼″	7-C small	1 square 4½″ × 4½″
Pea Soup	7-D large	1 square 5¼″ × 5¼″	7-D small	1 square 4½″ × 4½″
Butternut Squash	Large circle	1 or 2 squares 5½″ × 5½″	Small circle	1 or 2 squares 5″ × 5″

Other supplies:

- Embroidery floss in assorted colors
- Batting or fiberfill
- Freezer paper

INSTRUCTIONS

Refer to Information for All Projects (page 9) for basic information on making and using templates and sewing.

1. Make the freezer-paper templates and cut the felt pieces.

2. Center circle 7-A on flower shape 7-B and sew together using a blanket stitch.

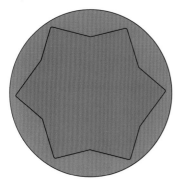

3. Center shape 7-D on the background circle and sew together using a whipstitch.

4. Center flower shape 7-C on the background unit as shown and sew together along the edge of flower shape 7-C using a whipstitch.

5. Center flower unit 7-A/B on the background unit and sew together along the edge of flower shape 7-B using a whipstitch.

6. Sew decorative stitches on flower unit 7-A/B using a lazy daisy stitch, running stitch, and French knots.

7. Sew decorative stitches on flower shape 7-C using a lazy daisy stitch and running stitch; sew French knots on shape 7-D.

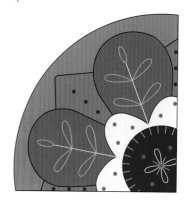

8. Refer to Using the Designs (page 8) for instructions and options to finish the project.

FLURRY

FINISHED ORNAMENTS
Large: 5″ diameter
Small: 4¼″ diameter

CHRISTMAS MEMORIES Kids' Trim-a-Tree Party

When our kids were in grade school we would have a trim-a-tree party each year. We would start with a craft for the kids to make, and the friends could take their crafts home to share with their families. Then our kids took their friends up to their bedrooms and they decorated the kids'

trees. We'd watch a classic Christmas video and decorate cookies, brownies, or cupcakes, and that became the snack. We'd finish up the evening with carols around the piano. The kids grow up so fast—be sure to make those great memories while you can.

MATERIALS

Refer to Color Options (page 6); for patterns, refer to Ornament Backgrounds (page 56) and Flurry patterns (page 64).

COLORS AND QUANTITY OF WOOL FELT				
COLOR	LARGE ORNAMENT		SMALL ORNAMENT	
	Pattern	Amount needed	Pattern	Amount needed
Pea Soup	8-A large	1 square 1½″ × 1½″	8-A small	1 square 1¼″ × 1¼″
Tropical Wave	8-B large	1 square 2″ × 2″	8-B small	1 square 1¾″ × 1¾″
Fresh Linen	8-C large	1 square 3¼″ × 3¼″	8-C small	1 square 3″ × 3″
Barnyard Red	8-D large	1 square 4″ × 4″	8-D small	1 square 3½″ × 3½″
Butternut Squash	8-E large	1 square 5″ × 5″	8- E small	1 square 4½″ × 4½″
Tropical Wave	Large circle	1 or 2 squares 5½″ × 5½″	Small circle	1 or 2 squares 5″ × 5″

Other supplies:

- Embroidery floss in assorted colors
- Batting or fiberfill
- Freezer paper

INSTRUCTIONS

Refer to Information for All Projects (page 9) for basic information on making and using templates and sewing.

1. Make the freezer-paper templates and cut the felt pieces.

2. Center circle 8-A on circle 8-B and sew together using a whipstitch.

3. Center the 8-A/B unit on flower shape 8-C and sew together along the edge of circle 8-B using a whipstitch.

4. Center shape 8-D on shape 8-E as shown. Be sure the pointed edges of 8-D are positioned in the scalloped edges of shape 8-E. Sew together using a whipstitch.

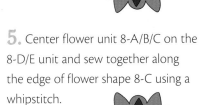

5. Center flower unit 8-A/B/C on the 8-D/E unit and sew together along the edge of flower shape 8-C using a whipstitch.

6. Center the 8-A/B/C/D/E unit on the background circle and sew together along the edge of shape 8-E using a whipstitch.

7. Sew decorative stitches in flower shape 8-A/B/C using a lazy daisy stitch, running stitch, and French knots.

8. Sew decorative stitches in shapes 8-D and 8-E using a lazy daisy stitch and French knots.

9. Refer to Using the Designs (page 8) for instructions and options to finish the project.

JINGLE

FINISHED ORNAMENTS
Large: 4⅞″ × 4⅞″
Small: 4⅛″ × 4⅛″

CHRISTMAS MEMORIES First Date under a Famous Christmas Tree

Mr. Wonderful and I met in college. Our school was located on a mountaintop overlooking New York City. Our first date took place in Manhattan. We went to dinner at Wo Hop in Chinatown and then to the famous Joe Allen Restaurant in the Theater District. We ended up at Rockefeller Center to see the big tree. Somehow Mr. Wonderful talked the guard into allowing us onto the closed ice rink located below the tree. We slipped and slid around in our shoes, and I think we both realized this was a pretty phenomenal first date. Now, all these years later, though we live far from New York, whenever we see the Rockefeller Center tree on television or in movies, we always smile.

MATERIALS

Refer to Color Options (page 6); for patterns, refer to Ornament Backgrounds (page 56) and Jingle patterns (page 65).

COLORS AND QUANTITY OF WOOL FELT				
COLOR	LARGE ORNAMENT		SMALL ORNAMENT	
	Pattern	Amount needed	Pattern	Amount needed
Butternut Squash	9-A large	1 square 1¼″ × 1¼″	9-A small	1 square 1″ × 1″
Fresh Linen	9-B large	1 square 2½″ × 2½″	9-B small	1 square 2½″ × 2½″
Tropical Wave	9-C large	1 square 3″ × 3″	9-C small	1 square 3″ × 3″
Pea Soup	9-D large	1 square 4½″ × 4½″	9-D small	1 square 4″ × 4″
Barnyard Red	Large square	1 or 2 squares 5½″ × 5½″	Small square	1 or 2 squares 5″ × 5″

Other supplies:

■ Embroidery floss in assorted colors

■ Batting or fiberfill

■ Freezer paper

INSTRUCTIONS

Refer to Information for All Projects (page 9) for basic information on making and using templates and sewing.

1. Make the freezer-paper templates and cut the felt pieces.

2. Center circle 9-A on shape 9-B and sew together using a whipstitch.

3. Center the 9-A/B unit on flower shape 9-C and sew together along the edge of shape 9-B using a whipstitch.

4. Center shape 9-D on the background square and sew together using a whipstitch.

5. Center flower unit 9-A/B/C on unit 9-D/E and sew together along the edge of flower shape 9-C using a whipstitch.

6. Sew decorative stitches in the flower shape using a running stitch and French knots.

7. Sew decorative stitches in shape 9-D using French knots.

8. Refer to Using the Designs (page 8) for instructions and options to finish the project.

MUG RUGS

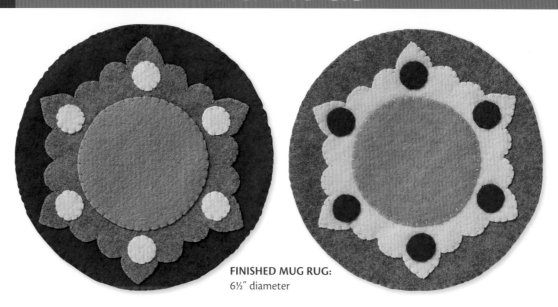

FINISHED MUG RUG:
6½" diameter

 What's nicer than cozying up by the fire, listening to some carols, and looking at the Christmas tree? It's only there for a short time, so be sure to enjoy it. Make some hot cocoa, add a candy cane (chocolate and peppermint—yum), and use one of these mug rugs to set your cup of cocoa on. They make great gifts for teachers, friends, and neighbors—place a mug rug in a cellophane bag and top it with a holiday mug filled with cocoa mix and candy canes.

MATERIALS

Refer to Color Options (page 6) and Mug Rug patterns (page 66).

COLORS AND QUANTITY OF WOOL FELT		
COLOR	PATTERN	AMOUNT NEEDED
Pea Soup	10-A	1 square 3¾" × 3¾"
Tropical Wave	10-B	1 square 6½" × 6½"
Fresh Linen	10-C	6 squares 1¼" × 1¼"
Barnyard Red	10-D	2 squares 7" × 7"

Other supplies:

- Embroidery floss in assorted colors
- Freezer paper

INSTRUCTIONS

Refer to Information for All Projects (page 9) for basic information on making and using templates and sewing.

1. Make the freezer-paper templates and cut the felt pieces.

2. Center circle 10-A on shape 10-B and sew together using a whipstitch.

3. Center the 10-A/B unit on circle 10-D and sew together along the edge of shape 10-B using a whipstitch.

4. Place a circle 10-C on each of the pointed shapes of shape 10-B and sew together using a whipstitch.

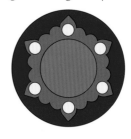

5. Place appliquéd circle 10-A/B/C/D on plain circle 10-D and sew together along the edge using a whipstitch.

Need a quick change of decor for the holidays? A simple fix is to change the throw pillows on your sofas or armchairs. Stitch a few up before the holidays and just toss!

FINISHED PILLOW: 20½″ × 20½″

MATERIALS

Refer to Color Options (page 6) and Pillow patterns (pages 66 and 67).

COLORS AND QUANTITY OF WOOL FELT

COLOR	PATTERN	AMOUNT NEEDED
Barnyard Red	11-A	1 square 7″ × 7″
Pea Soup	11-B	1 square 4½″ × 4½″
Tropical Wave	11-C	1 square 2¾″ × 2¾″
Barnyard Red	11-D	4 squares 5″ × 5″
Pea Soup	11-E	4 squares 2½″ × 2½″
Pea Soup	11-F	4 squares 2½″ × 2½″
Tropical Wave	11-G	4 squares 3″ × 3″
Fresh Linen	11-H	5 squares 1¾″ × 1¾″
Butternut Squash	11-I	5 squares 1½″ × 1½″
Fresh Linen	Background	1 square 14″ × 14″

COLORS, QUANTITY, AND CUTTING FOR COTTON FABRIC

FABRIC	AMOUNT NEEDED	CUTTING		
		For	Strips to cut	Subcut
Red print	1¼ yards	Borders	2 strips 2½″ × WOF*	2 strips 2½″ × 14″
				2 strips 2½″ × 16½″
		Ruffle	3 strips 6½″ × WOF	—
		Pillow back	1 strip 12½″ × WOF	2 rectangles 12½″ × 16½″

* WOF = width of fabric

Other supplies:

- Embroidery floss in assorted colors
- Freezer paper
- Quilting thread or other heavy thread
- 16″ × 16″ pillow form

INSTRUCTIONS

Refer to Information for All Projects (page 9) for basic information on making and using templates and sewing.

FELT CENTER

1. Fold the 14" × 14" background square on the diagonal and press; then fold diagonally from the opposite corners and press. Using a single strand of thread, baste along the pressed lines using a long running stitch. Press again to remove the creases.

2. Make the freezer-paper templates and cut the felt pieces.

3. Center shape 11-A on the background square. (Use the basting stitches to help center the shape; the inner points should be placed along a basting line.) Sew together using a whipstitch.

4. Center circle 11-I on circle 11-H and sew together using a whipstitch. Make 5 of these units.

Make 5.

5. Center flower shape 11-C on shape 11-B and sew together using a whipstitch.

6. Center a circle unit 11-H/I on unit 11-B/C and sew together along the edge of circle 11-H using a whipstitch.

7. Center the 11-B/C/H/I unit on shape 11-A, aligning 4 of the points of shape 11-B with the basting lines as shown. Sew together using a whipstitch along the edge of shape 11-B.

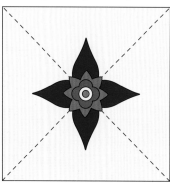

8. Center a leaf shape 11-E in the left leaf area of shape 11-D and sew together using a whipstitch. Center a leaf shape 11-F in the right leaf area of shape 11-D and sew together using a whipstitch. Repeat for all 4 of the 11-D shapes.

9. Center heart shape 11-G in the bottom part of the 11-D unit and sew together using a whipstitch around heart shape 11-G. Repeat for all 4 units.

10. Place circle unit 11-H/I on the 11-D/E/F/G unit as shown and sew together using a whipstitch around circle unit 11-H/I. Repeat for all 4 units.

11. Place the 11-D/E/F/G/H/I unit in the corner of the background square so that the bottom point of the unit is 2" from the corner of the square and is aligned with the basting stitches. Sew together using a whipstitch around the 11-D/E/F/G/H/I unit. Repeat in each corner.

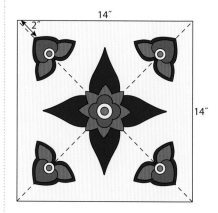

MAKING THE PILLOW

Seam allowances are ⅝".

1. Sew a 2½" × 14" strip to each side of the felt square. Press the seams toward the strips. Sew 2½" × 16½" strips to the top and bottom of the felt square. Press the seams toward the strips to make the pillow front.

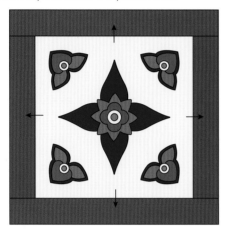

2. Trim the selvage ends from the 6½" × width of fabric strips. Sew the 3 strips together along the short ends to make a large loop and press the seams open. Fold the loop in half with wrong sides together and press.

3. Sew gathering stitches along the loop, about ½" from the raw edges all the way around. I do this by sewing a large zigzag stitch over a strong thread, such as quilting thread. Secure the end of the thread with a pin so that it does not pull through while sewing.

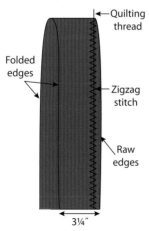

4. Divide the loop into 4 equal parts and pin at each corner of the pillow front. Be sure to secure the ends of the gathering thread; then pull up the thread to gather the ruffle. Align the gathered edge of the ruffle with the raw edges of the borders. Pin the ruffle all the way around the edge, distributing the gathers evenly. Machine baste ⅜" from the edge.

5. On a long edge of each of the 12½" × 16½" rectangles, turn under ½" and press; turn under ½" again and stitch in place.

6. Place the rectangles right sides together with the pillow front, aligning the raw edges of the rectangles with the raw edges of the pillow front. The rectangles will overlap in the center. Pin in place and stitch around the edges, overlapping the stitching and backstitching at the beginning and end.

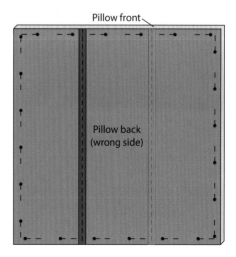

7. Turn the pillow right side out and, with a seam ripper, remove any basting stitches that show. Insert the pillow form.

CANDLE MAT AND COZY

Candle Mat

MATERIALS

Refer to Color Options (page 6) and Candle Mat patterns (page 68).

COLORS AND QUANTITY OF WOOL FELT		
COLOR	PATTERN	AMOUNT NEEDED
Pea Soup	12-A	1 square 5½″ × 5½″
Fresh Linen	12-B	8 squares 2¾″ × 2¾″
Barnyard Red	12-C	8 squares 2½″ × 2½″
Tropical Wave	12-D	2 squares 9½″ × 9½″

Other supplies:

- Embroidery floss in assorted colors
- Freezer paper

FINISHED CANDLE MAT: 9″ diameter
FINISHED CANDLE COZY: 5½″ tall with a 12½″ circumference as shown (it will be customized to fit your candle jar)

Want to set the mood for the holiday? Light some candles and turn off all the lights except for the Christmas lights. Set a couple of these candle mats and cozies on the dining table and dine by candlelight. Don't forget the Christmas cookies for dessert!

INSTRUCTIONS

Refer to Information for All Projects (page 9) for basic information on making and using templates and sewing.

1. Make the freezer-paper templates and cut the felt pieces. *Note: Fold a 10" square of freezer paper in quarters with the dull side out; trace pattern 12-D onto freezer paper as indicated on the pattern to make the template.*

2. Center circle 12-A on scallop shape 12-D and sew together using a whipstitch.

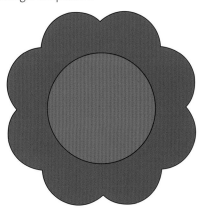

3. Center shape 12-C on shape 12-B and sew together using a whipstitch. Make 8 of this unit.

4. Center a 12-B/C unit in each of the scallops of unit 12-A/D and sew together using a whipstitch around the edges of each 12-B/C unit.

5. Place an appliquéd 12-D unit on top of the plain 12-D shape and sew together along the edge using a whipstitch.

Candle Cozy

MATERIALS

Refer to Color Options (page 6) and Candle Cozy patterns (page 69).

COLORS AND QUANTITY OF WOOL FELT		
COLOR	PATTERN	AMOUNT NEEDED
Fresh Linen	13-A	1 rectangle 2" × 15"
Pea Soup	13-B	3 squares 1¾" × 1¾"
Tropical Wave	13-B	2 squares 1¾" × 1¾"
Fresh Linen	13-B	2 squares 1¾" × 1¾"
Tropical Wave	13-C	5 squares 1" × 1"
Fresh Linen	13-C	4 squares 1" × 1"
Barnyard Red	13-C	3 squares 1" × 1"
Pea Soup	13-C	2 squares 1" × 1"
Barnyard Red	Background*	2 rectangles 8" × 15"

* Refer to Candle Cozy Instructions, Step 1 (page 36), to determine the exact size needed.

Other supplies:

■ Embroidery floss in assorted colors
■ Freezer paper
■ Glass candle jar*

* It's best to use a candle jar with straight sides rather than one with curves or indentations. The jar I used is 5½" tall and has a circumference of 12½".

INSTRUCTIONS

Refer to Information for All Projects (page 9) for basic information on making and using templates and sewing.

1. Make the freezer-paper templates and cut the felt pieces.

- To cut the background, first measure the circumference of the jar and add ½"—this will be the horizontal measurement of the rectangle. Measure from the bottom of the jar to 1" below the top—this will be the vertical measurement of the rectangle. Cut 2 rectangles to this size.

- Fold a 1½" × 15" piece of freezer paper in half and trace pattern 13-A as indicated on the pattern to make a template. After cutting 2 of these shapes from felt, trim them to fit the length measurement of the background rectangle.

2. Place the 13-A borders on the long edges of the background rectangle and sew together along the zigzag edge of the border strips using a whipstitch. Do not sew along the straight edges yet; that will come later. In each of the triangles of the borders, stitch a French knot.

3. Center a circle 13-C on a circle 13-B and sew together using a whipstitch. Make a total of 7 in the color combinations shown.

Make 3.   Make 2.   Make 2.

4. Arrange the circles 13-B/C and 13-C on the background rectangle as shown and sew together using a whipstitch. Place the circles at least ¾" away from each of the short sides to allow for sewing a seam.

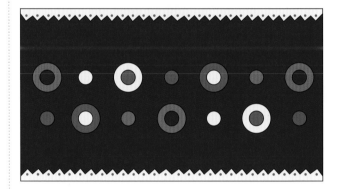

5. Place the appliquéd rectangle on top of the plain rectangle and sew together along the top and bottom edges using a whipstitch.

6. Place the rectangle around the jar with the plain side facing out. Align the short raw edges of the background and pin them together next to the candle. Carefully slip the cozy off the jar and sew next to the pins using a running stitch; make your stitches as short as possible. Stitch again to reinforce the seam. Trim the seam allowance to ¼" if necessary. Turn right side out and slide the cozy over the candle jar.

FINISHED TABLE TOPPER: 17½″ × 17½″

Be sure to decorate all through the house! This table topper is versatile— it can decorate the center of the dining table, an end table in the living room, or even a bedside table to add Christmas cheer to a bedroom.

INSTRUCTIONS

Refer to Information for All Projects (page 9) for basic information on making and using templates and sewing.

1. Make the freezer-paper templates and cut the felt pieces.

■ *To make a freezer-paper template for shape 14-J, fold a 12″ square of freezer paper in half with the dull side out. Place the pattern on the folded edge of the freezer paper and trace as indicated on the pattern.*

■ *To make a freezer-paper template for background piece 14-K, fold an 18″ square of freezer paper in quarters with the dull side out. Trace pattern 14-K onto freezer paper as indicated on the pattern.*

2. Center circle 14-A on circle 14-B and sew together using a whipstitch.

Make 4.

3. Center circle 14-C on circle 14-D and sew together using a whipstitch.

Make 4.

4. Center circle 14-E on circle 14-F and sew together using a whipstitch.

5. Center circle unit 14-A/B on shape 14-G and sew together along the edge of circle 14-B using a whipstitch.

Make 4.

MATERIALS

Refer to Color Options (page 6) and Table Topper patterns (pages 69–71).

COLORS AND QUANTITY OF WOOL FELT		
COLOR	PATTERN	AMOUNT NEEDED
Tropical Wave	14-A	4 squares 1″ × 1″
Fresh Linen	14-B	4 squares 1½″ × 1½″
Fresh Linen	14-C	4 squares 1¼″ × 1¼″
Barnyard Red	14-D	4 squares 1¾″ × 1¾″
Tropical Wave	14-E	1 square 2″ × 2″
Fresh Linen	14-F	1 square 2½″ × 2½″
Barnyard Red	14-G	4 squares 2¾″ × 2¾″
Barnyard Red	14-H	1 square 4½″ × 4½″
Tropical Wave	14-I	4 rectangles 5″ × 6½″
Pea Soup	14-J	1 square 10″ × 10″
Fresh Linen	14-K	1 square 17″ × 17″
Barnyard Red	Background	2 squares 17½″ × 17½″

Other supplies:

■ Embroidery floss in assorted colors

■ Freezer paper

6. Place circle unit 14-C/D on shape 14-I as shown and sew together along the edge of circle 14-D using a whipstitch.

Make 4.

7. Center circle unit 14-E/F on shape 14-H and sew together along the edge of circle 14-F using a whipstitch.

8. Center shape 14-K on one of the 17½" background squares and sew together using a whipstitch.

9. Fold the square on the diagonal and press; fold on the diagonal from the opposite corners and press. Using a single strand of thread, make large running stitches along the folds. Press again to remove the creases. Fold the square in half and press; open and fold the square in half in the other direction and press. Using a single strand of thread, make large running stitches along the folds. Press again to remove the creases. The thread lines will help you to arrange your design evenly.

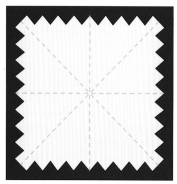

10. Place shape 14-J on the background unit using the basting stitches to align and center the shape. Sew along all the edges of shape 14-J using a whipstitch.

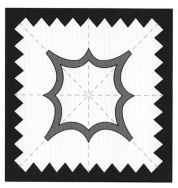

11. Place the 14-C/D/I unit on the background as shown, so the point of the unit is 1⅞" from the edge of shape 14-K. Sew together using a whipstitch. Repeat for each corner.

12. Place the 14-E/F/H unit in the center of the background and sew together using a whipstitch.

13. Place the bottom inner point of the 14-A/B/G unit on the point of shape 14-J as shown and sew together using a whipstitch. Repeat for all 4 units.

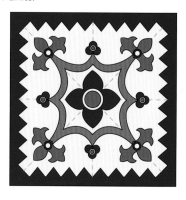

14. Remove the basting stitches. Place the appliquéd background square on the plain square and sew together along the edges using a whipstitch.

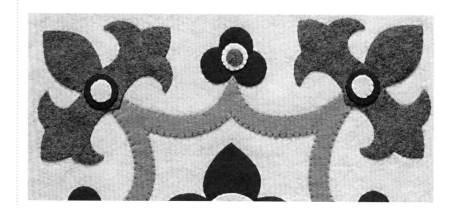

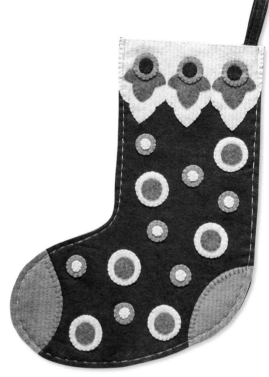

FINISHED STOCKING: 11″ × 14″

 I sometimes think buying and opening all the little presents for the stockings is more fun than the big gifts. I love the art supplies, the sewing notions, the cosmetics, and of course the candy that we find in our stockings. No matter how old we are, it seems we still love stocking stuffers.

MATERIALS

Refer to Color Options (page 6) and Stocking patterns (pages 72–74).

COLORS AND QUANTITY OF WOOL FELT		
COLOR	PATTERN	AMOUNT NEEDED
Barnyard Red	15-A	3 squares 1¼″ × 1¼″
Pea Soup	15-B	3 squares 1¾″ × 1¾″
Tropical Wave	15-C	6 squares 1½″ × 1½″
Pea Soup	15-C	7 squares 1½″ × 1½″
Fresh Linen	15-D	6 squares 2″ × 2″
Fresh Linen	15-E	7 squares 1″ × 1″
Tropical Wave	15-F	3 rectangles 2″ × 2½″
Pea Soup	15-G	1 rectangle 3″ × 5″
Pea Soup	15-H	1 rectangle 2½″ × 5″
Fresh Linen	15-I	1 rectangle 4½″ × 7″
Barnyard Red	15-J	2 rectangles 12″ × 15″
Barnyard Red	Hanger	1 rectangle 1″ × 6″

Other supplies:

- Embroidery floss in assorted colors
- Freezer paper

INSTRUCTIONS

Refer to Information for All Projects (page 9) for basic information on making and using templates and sewing.

1. Make the freezer-paper templates and cut the felt pieces. Label the pieces as you cut and keep them organized by size.

■ *To make the stocking pattern, cut a 12" × 16" piece of freezer paper. Join the 3 parts of the pattern when tracing onto freezer paper. You'll need to tape 2 sheets together if you're using the smaller sheets of freezer paper.*

2. Center circle 15-A on circle 15-B and sew together using a whipstitch.

Make 3.

3. Center circle 15-E on circle 15-C and sew together using a whipstitch.

Make 7.

4. Center circle 15-C on circle 15-D and sew together using a whipstitch.

Make 6.

5. Place 3 of the 15-F shapes on 15-I as shown. Sew together using a whipstitch.

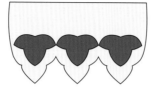

6. Place the 15-A/B circle units on the 15-I unit as shown and sew together along the edge of circle 15-B using a whipstitch.

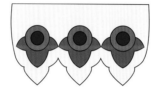

7. Place shape 15-G in the toe of one of the 15-J stocking shapes and shape 15-H in the heel of the stocking shape, positioning them so the outside edges align with the curves, and pin in place. Sew the inner curves of each shape to the stocking using a blanket stitch. Do not sew the outer curves at this time.

8. Place the 15-A/C/F/I unit along the top of the stocking front, matching the sides and top, and sew together using a whipstitch along all the edges.

9. Place the 6 circle shapes 15-C/D on the stocking and sew together along the edge of circle 15-D using a whipstitch.

10. Place the 7 circle shapes 15-C/E on the stocking as shown and sew together along the edge of circle 15-C using a whipstitch.

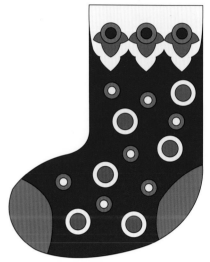

Appliquéd stocking

11. Place the appliquéd stocking over the plain stocking and pin together along the edges. Leaving the top open, machine stitch ¼" from the edge, being sure to lock the stitches at the beginning and end. Using a ¼" running stitch, hand sew over the machine stitching.

12. To make a hanger, press the 1" × 6" strip of felt in half lengthwise. Machine stitch ⅛" from each side. Fold in half and hand sew to the inside of the plain stocking.

FINISHED QUILT: 29½" × 29½"

This is a sweet little project that would look fabulous hanging above the mantel for the holidays. It combines quilting with hand-stitched felt. Settle in by the fire and stitch the nine ornament designs to feature in this charming quilt. I like alternating the circle and square backgrounds.

MATERIALS AND CUTTING

FABRIC COLORS, QUANTITY, AND CUTTING DETAILS				
FABRIC	AMOUNT NEEDED	CUTTING		
		For	Strips to cut	Subcut
Fabric A (white print)	⅝ yard	Block backgrounds	2 strips 6½″ × WOF*	9 squares 6½″ × 6½″
Fabric B (green print)	⅓ yard	Sashing	4 strips 2″ × WOF	24 rectangles 2″ × 6½″
Fabric C (red print)	⅛ yard	Sashing cornerstones	1 strip 2″ × WOF	16 squares 2″ × 2″
Fabric D (blue print)	½ yard	Border	4 strips 3″ × WOF	—
Binding	⅜ yard	Binding	4 strips 2¼″ × WOF	—
Backing	1 yard			
Batting	35″ × 35″			

WOF = width of fabric

Other supplies:

- Wool felt for 9 large-size ornaments
- Embroidery floss in assorted colors
- Freezer paper

INSTRUCTIONS

Seam allowances are ¼″.

APPLIQUÉ DESIGNS

Follow the instructions to make the 9 ornament designs, using the patterns for the larger size. You will need just 1 background square or circle for each.

QUILT CENTER

1. Arrange 3 blocks and 4 sashing rectangles in a row as shown and sew together. Press the seams toward the sashing. Make 3 rows.

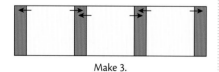

Make 3.

2. Arrange 3 sashing rectangles and 4 cornerstones in a row as shown and sew together. Press the seams toward the sashing. Make 4 rows.

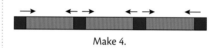

Make 4.

3. Arrange the sashing rows and block rows and sew together. Press the seams toward the block rows.

BORDERS

1. Measure from top to bottom through the middle of the quilt and cut 2 strips to this measurement. Sew the strips to the sides of the quilt. Press the seams toward the borders.

2. Measure from side to side through the middle of the quilt, including the borders. Cut 2 strips to this measurement. Sew the strips to the top and bottom. Press the seams toward the borders.

FINISHING

1. Layer the backing, batting, and top. Quilt as desired.

2. Trim and sew together the binding strips to make 1 long strip. Bind as desired.

3. Center a felt design in each of the white print blocks and sew to the quilt using a whipstitch.

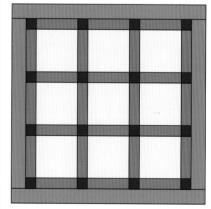

Quilt assembly

FINISHED BLOCKS: 14″ × 14″
FINISHED QUILT: 62½″ × 78½″

The blocks in this jewel-like quilt will look like colorful snowflakes inside your house. The quilt would look great on the wall as a backdrop to the tree. It would also make a lovely quilt to cuddle under on the couch.

MATERIALS AND CUTTING

Note: If you cut all your fabric at once, I suggest that you pin labels to the cut pieces indicating where the pieces will be used. Or, if you prefer, you can cut the fabric as you go.

FABRIC COLORS, QUANTITY, AND CUTTING DETAILS

FABRIC	AMOUNT NEEDED	CUTTING		
		For	Strips to cut	Subcut
Fabric A (white batik print)	2 yards	Block 1	4 strips 2½″ × WOF*	24 rectangles 2½″ × 6½″
			3 strips 2½″ × WOF	48 squares 2½″ × 2½″
			2 strips 3¼″ × WOF	24 squares 3¼″ × 3¼″
		Block 2	4 strips 2½″ × WOF	24 rectangles 2½″ × 6½″
			3 strips 2½″ × WOF	48 squares 2½″ × 2½″
			2 strips 3¼″ × WOF	24 squares 3¼″ × 3¼″
Fabric B (red batik print)	1¼ yards	Middle border	5 strips 3¼″ × WOF	60 squares 3¼″ × 3¼″
		Block 1	5 strips 2½″ × WOF	72 squares 2½″ × 2½″
		Block 2	3 strips 2½″ × WOF	48 squares 2½″ × 2½″
			2 strips 3¼″ × WOF	24 squares 3¼″ × 3¼″
		Middle border	3 strips 3¼″ × WOF	30 squares 3¼″ × 3¼″
Fabric C (turquoise batik print)	1¼ yards	Block 1	3 strips 2½″ × WOF	48 squares 2½″ × 2½″
			2 strips 3¼″ × WOF	24 squares 3¼″ × 3¼″
		Block 2	5 strips 2½″ × WOF	72 squares 2½″ × 2½″
		Middle border	3 strips 3¼″ × WOF	30 squares 3¼″ × 3¼″
Fabric D (gold batik print)	¼ yard	Blocks 1 and 2	1 strip 2½″ × WOF	12 squares 2½″ × 2½″
		Sashing cornerstones	1 strip 2½″ × WOF	6 squares 2½″ × 2½″
		Middle border	1 strip 2½″ × WOF	4 squares 2½″ × 2½″
Fabric E (green batik print)	2¼ yards	Sashing	9 strips 2½″ × WOF	17 strips 2½″ × 14½″
		Inner border	6 strips 3½″ × WOF	—
		Outer border	7 strips 3½″ × WOF	—
Binding	⅝ yard	Binding	8 strips 2¼″ × WOF	—
Backing	2 yards of 108″-wide fabric *or* 4⅞ yards of 40″-wide fabric			
Batting	71″ × 87″			

* WOF = width of fabric

INSTRUCTIONS

Seam allowances are ¼".

HALF-SQUARE TRIANGLES

For most efficient piecing, make all the half-square triangle units at once for Block 1, Block 2, and the pieced middle border.

1. Mark a diagonal line from corner to corner on the wrong side of each of 24 Fabric A 3¼" squares.

2. Pair the 24 Fabric A squares with Fabric C 3¼" squares, right sides together. On each pair, sew ¼" from each side of the drawn line.

3. Cut on each drawn line. Press the seams toward Fabric C.

4. Square each half-square triangle unit to 2½" × 2½". You'll have 48 units for Block 1.

Make 48.

5. Repeat Steps 1–4, but pair 24 Fabric A squares with Fabric B squares to make 48 units for Block 2. Press the seams toward Fabric B.

Make 48.

---

6. Repeat Steps 1–4, pairing 30 Fabric A squares with Fabric C squares and 30 Fabric A squares with Fabric B squares to make 60 units of each for the pieced middle border. Press the seams of the A/C units toward Fabric A and press the seams of the A/B units toward Fabric B, so that they will nest together when you piece the border.

Make 60 of each.

BLOCK 1

Corner Units

1. Arrange the 2½" squares of Fabrics A, B, and C with the half-square triangle units in 3 rows as shown and sew together. Press the seams in Rows 1 and 3 toward the outside and the seams in Row 2 toward the inside.

2. Stitch the rows together and press the seams open to reduce bulk. The corner unit should measure 6½" × 6½".

Block 1 corner unit—make 24.

Block 1 Assembly

1. Arrange 4 corner units, 4 Fabric A 2½" × 6½" rectangles, and 1 Fabric D 2½" square as shown. Refer to the diagram below to make sure the corner units are oriented correctly (Fabric A pieces should always be along the outer edge).

2. Stitch the units together in 3 rows. Press the seams in Rows 1 and 3 to the outside and the seams in Row 2 to the inside.

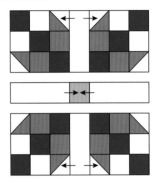

3. Stitch the rows together. Press the seams open to reduce bulk. The block should measure 14½" × 14½".

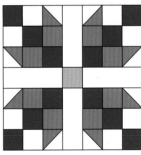

Block 1—make 6.

BLOCK 2

Corner Units

1. Arrange the 2½" squares of Fabrics A, B, and C with the half-square triangle units in 3 rows as shown and sew together. Press the seams in Rows 1 and 3 toward the outside and the seams in Row 2 toward the inside.

2. Stitch the rows together and press the seams open to reduce bulk. The corner unit should measure 6½" × 6½".

Block 2 corner unit—make 24.

Block 2 Assembly

1. Arrange 4 corner units, 4 Fabric A 2½" × 6½" rectangles, and 1 Fabric D 2½" square as shown. Refer to the diagram below to make sure the corner units are oriented correctly (Fabric A pieces should be along the outer edge).

2. Stitch the units together in 3 rows. Press the seams in Rows 1 and 3 to the outside and the seams in Row 2 to the inside.

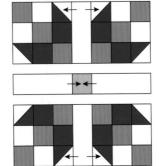

3. Stitch the rows together. Press the seams open to reduce bulk. The block should measure 14½" × 14½".

Block 2—make 6.

QUILT TOP ASSEMBLY

Refer to the quilt assembly diagram (next page) as needed.

Quilt Center

1. Arrange and sew 2 of Block 1, 1 of Block 2, and 2 sashing strips to make a row as shown. Press the seams toward the sashing. Repeat with 1 of Block 1, 2 of Block 2, and 2 sashing strips to make a row as shown. Make 2 of each row.

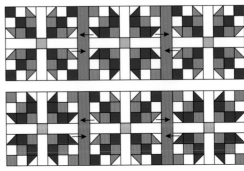

Make 2 of each.

2. Sew the Fabric D squares and sashing strips together as shown. Press the seams toward the sashing. Make 3 rows.

Make 3.

3. Arrange the 4 rows of sashing and blocks with the 3 rows of sashing and cornerstones as shown in the quilt assembly diagram. Pin and stitch the rows together, matching seams. Press the seams toward the cornerstone/sashing rows.

Inner Border

1. Trim the selvage ends from the inner border strips and stitch together end to end to make 1 long strip.

2. Measure the quilt top from top to bottom through the middle. Cut 2 strips from the long strip to this length. Sew a strip to each side of the quilt.

3. Measure the quilt top from side to side through the middle, including the borders you just added. Cut 2 strips from the long strip to this length. Stitch the strips to the top and bottom of the quilt top.

Middle Border

1. Arrange 13 Fabric A/B and 13 Fabric A/C half-square triangle units with 2 Fabric D 2½″ squares as shown and sew together. Arrange 17 Fabric A/B and 17 Fabric A/C half-square triangle units as shown and sew together. Make 2 of each border strip.

Make 2 of each.

2. Sew the longer border strips to the sides of the quilt with the Fabric A triangles on the outer edge. Press the seams toward the inner border.

3. Sew the shorter border strips to the top and bottom with the Fabric A triangles on the outer edge. Press the seams toward the inner border.

Outer Border

1. Trim the selvage ends from the outer border strips and stitch together end to end to make 1 long strip.

2. Measure the quilt top from top to bottom through the middle. Cut 2 strips from the long strip to this length. Sew a strip to each side of the quilt.

3. Measure the quilt top from side to side through the middle, including the borders you just added. Cut 2 strips from the long strip to this length. Stitch the strips to the top and bottom of the quilt.

Quilt assembly

FINISHING

1. Layer the backing, batting, and quilt top. Quilt as desired.

2. Sew the binding strips together to make 1 long strip. Bind as desired.

QUILTED TABLE RUNNER

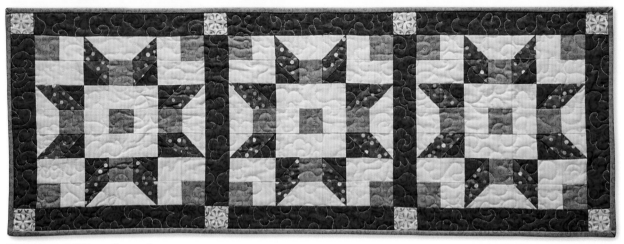

FINISHED BLOCKS: 10½″ × 10½″
FINISHED RUNNER: 14″ × 38″

 Here's a perfect addition to your holiday decor. This table runner isn't too big, so you can fit plates or placemats on the table with it. Add some greenery, pinecones, and candles and you're ready to entertain.

MATERIALS AND CUTTING

Note: If you cut all your fabric at once, I suggest that you pin labels to the cut pieces indicating where the pieces will be used. Or, if you prefer, you can cut the fabric as you go.

FABRIC COLORS, QUANTITY, AND CUTTING DETAILS				
		CUTTING		
FABRIC	**AMOUNT NEEDED**	*For*	*Strips to cut*	*Subcut*
Fabric A (white-on-white print)	½ yard	Blocks	4 strips 2″ × WOF*	48 squares 2″ × 2″
				12 rectangles 2″ × 3½″
			1 strip 2¾″ × WOF	12 squares 2¾″ × 2¾″
Fabric B (red tone-on-tone print)	½ yard	Blocks	1 strip 2¾″ × WOF	12 squares 2¾″ × 2¾″
		Sashing	4 strips 2″ × WOF	10 strips 2″ × 11″
Fabric C (blue print)	¼ yard	Blocks	2 strips 2¾″ × WOF	24 squares 2¾″ × 2¾″
Fabric D (green print)	¼ yard	Blocks	2 strips 2″ × WOF	27 squares 2″ × 2″
Fabric E (light blue print)	⅛ yard	Sashing cornerstones	1 strip 2″ × WOF**	8 squares 2″ × 2″
Binding	⅓ yard	Binding	3 strips 2¼″ × WOF	—
Backing	1⅓ yards			
Batting	22″ × 46″			

* WOF = width of fabric   ** *Note that I fussy cut the sashing squares from the light blue print. You may not want to cut a strip first if you decide to fussy cut the squares.*

INSTRUCTIONS

Seam allowances are ¼".

HALF-SQUARE TRIANGLES

1. Mark a diagonal line from corner to corner on the wrong side of each of the Fabric C 2¾" squares.

2. Pair the marked squares right sides together with 12 Fabric A 2¾" squares and 12 Fabric B 2¾" squares so you have 12 A/C pairs and 12 B/C pairs.

3. On each pair, stitch ¼" from each side of the drawn line.

4. Cut on each drawn line and press all the seams toward Fabric C. Trim and square each half-square triangle unit to 2" × 2".

Make 24 of each.

BLOCK UNITS

1. Arrange 2 Fabric A/B and 2 Fabric A/C half-square triangle units with 2 Fabric A 2" squares, 1 Fabric A 2" × 3½" rectangle, and 1 Fabric D 2" square in 3 rows as shown and stitch together. Press the seams in Rows 1 and 3 toward the outside and the seam in Row 2 toward the inside.

2. Stitch together the rows and press the seams toward the outside. The unit should measure 5" × 5".

3. Repeat Steps 1 and 2 to make 12 corner units.

Corner unit—make 12.

4. Arrange 2 Fabric A 2" squares and 1 Fabric D 2" square as shown and stitch together. Press the seams to the inside. Make 12.

Center unit—make 12.

BLOCK ASSEMBLY

1. Arrange 4 corner units, 4 center units, and 1 Fabric D 2" square. Be sure to rotate the corner units so the Fabric D square is always in the outer corner. Stitch the units together in 3 rows. Press the seams in Rows 1 and 3 toward the inside and the seams in Row 2 toward the outside.

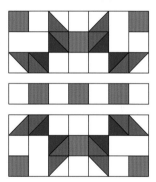

2. Stitch the rows together. Press the seams open to reduce bulk. The block should measure 11" × 11".

3. Repeat Steps 1 and 2 to make 3 blocks.

Make 3.

TABLE RUNNER ASSEMBLY

Refer to the runner assembly diagram (below) as needed.

1. Arrange the 3 blocks and 4 sashing strips in a row. Stitch together and press the seams toward the sashing strips.

2. Arrange the sashing strips and cornerstones to make the top and bottom strips and stitch together. Press the seams toward the sashing strips.

Make 2.

3. Sew the strips to the top and bottom of the runner. Press the seams open to reduce bulk.

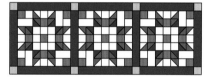

Runner assembly

FINISHING

1. Layer the backing, batting, and quilt top. Quilt as desired.

2. Sew the binding strips together to make 1 long strip. Bind as desired.

TREE SKIRT

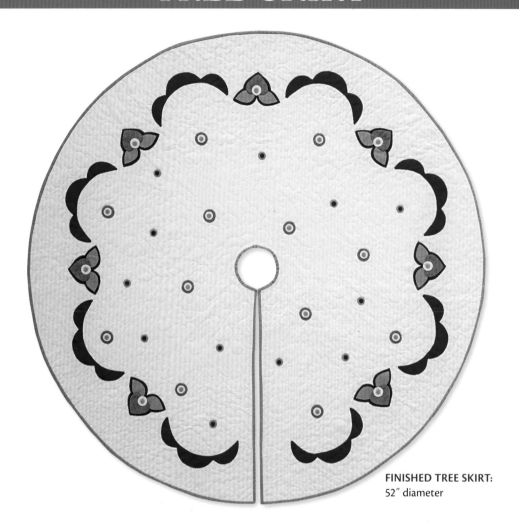

FINISHED TREE SKIRT:
52″ diameter

Of course, a decorated Christmas tree is pretty enough on its own, but this wonderful quilted tree skirt with wool felt appliqués will make your tree look even lovelier. The white background allows both the tree and the felt designs to stand out.

MATERIALS AND CUTTING

FABRIC COLORS, QUANTITY, AND CUTTING DETAILS			
FABRIC	AMOUNT NEEDED	FOR	CUTTING
Fabric A (white-on-white print)	3⅛ yards of 40″- to 44″-wide fabric *or* 1⅝ yards of 108″-wide fabric	Tree skirt background	Follow instructions in Cutting (next page).
Binding (green print)	⅔ yard for bias binding* *or* ½ yard for straight-grain binding	Binding	2¼″-wide bias strips to total 240″ *or* 6 strips 2¼″ × width of fabric
Backing	3¼ yards of 40″- to 44″-wide fabric *or* 1⅔ yards of 108″-wide fabric		
Batting	58″ × 58″		

* Bias binding will be easier to sew to the curved edges of the tree skirt, but straight-grain strips can be used if you prefer.

Refer to Color Options (page 6) and Tree Skirt patterns (page 75).

COLORS AND QUANTITY OF WOOL FELT		
COLOR	PATTERN	AMOUNT NEEDED
Barnyard Red	19-A	8 rectangles 5½" × 10"
Barnyard Red	19-B	7 rectangles 4½" × 6"
Tropical Wave	19-C	7 rectangles 3" × 3¼"
Pea Soup	19-D	7 rectangles 2" × 3"
Pea Soup	19-E	7 rectangles 2" × 3"
Fresh Linen	19-F	7 squares 1¾" × 1¾"
Tropical Wave	19-G	12 squares 2" × 2"
Fresh Linen	19-H	12 squares 1½" × 1½"
Pea Soup	19-H	12 squares 1½" × 1½"
Butternut Squash	19-I	19 squares 1" × 1"
Barnyard Red	19-I	12 squares 1" × 1"

Other supplies:
- Embroidery floss in assorted colors
- Freezer paper

CUTTING

1. For fabric that is 40"–44" wide, cut the yardage in half so that you have 2 pieces approximately 56" × 42". Remove the selvage edges and sew together to make a piece approximately 56" × 82". Press the seam allowances to one side and trim to 56" × 56" square, keeping the seam centered.

or

For extra-wide fabric, press the fabric and cut a square 56" × 56".

2. Open up the fabric, fold it in half, and then fold it in half again so that it is folded into quarters. Press the layers flat.

3. Place the end of a tape measure in the corner without raw edges and mark 26" out from the corner repeatedly to create an arc from one edge to the other. Connect the marks with a curved line. Cut on the line through all the layers to create the circle for the tree skirt.

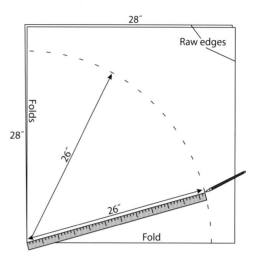

4. Repeat Step 1 for the backing fabric, cutting a square 58" × 58".

5. Cut the backing and the batting about 2" larger all around than the Fabric A circle.

INSTRUCTIONS
QUILTED TREE SKIRT

1. Press the fabrics well and layer and baste the backing, batting, and Fabric A circle. Quilt as desired.

2. Trim along the edge of the Fabric A circle after quilting.

3. Fold the quilted circle in quarters and mark the center.

4. Cut from edge of the circle to the center along one of the fold lines.

5. Measure around the trunk of your tree.

6. Open the quilted circle and mark a circle in the center using a circle template, a glass, or a bowl just a bit bigger than the size of the tree trunk.

7. Cut out the center circle.

8. Bind all the edges of the tree skirt.

APPLIQUÉ

Refer to Using Felt (page 6) and Information for All Projects (page 9) for basic information, including making and using templates.

1. Make the freezer-paper templates and cut the felt pieces.

2. Center a circle 19-I on a circle 19-F and sew together using a whipstitch.

Make 7.

3. Center a circle 19-I on a circle 19-H and sew together using a whipstitch. Refer to the illustration for the appropriate color combinations.

Make 12 of each.

4. Center a 19-H/I unit on a circle 19-G and sew together using a whipstitch.

Make 12.

5. Center a leaf shape 19-D on the left side of shape 19-B and sew together using a whipstitch. Repeat with leaf shape 19-E on the right side of shape 19-B.

Make 7.

6. Center heart shape 19-C in the lower part of the 19-B unit and sew together around the edges of heart shape 19-C using a whipstitch.

Make 7.

7. Place circle 19-F/I on the 19-B unit as shown and sew together around the edges of circle 19-F using a whipstitch.

Make 7.

8. Fold the tree skirt in half along the opening from edge to center and place a pin along the outer edge at the fold to mark the halfway point. Fold in half again and place a pin along the edge at each of the folds.

9. Open the tree skirt and add a pin between each of the previous pins by folding from pin to pin and adding the new pin at the fold. You should have a total of 7 pins around the outer edge.

10. Place a 19-B unit 4½" from the edge at each of the pins and sew to the quilt using a whipstitch. Catch only the top fabric and some of the

batting with the stitch—do not go through to the backing.

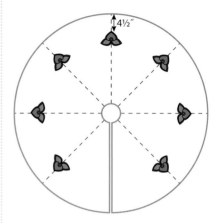

11. Center a swag shape 19-A between each of the 19-B units, placing the center bottom 2¾" from the edge of the quilt. Sew to the quilt using a whipstitch, catching only the top fabric and some of the batting.

12. Scatter the 12 circle units 19-G/H/I in the central area of the tree skirt, positioning them so they are evenly spaced. Sew to the quilt using a whipstitch, catching only the top fabric and some of the batting as before.

13. Scatter the 12 circle units 19-H/I in the central area of the tree skirt, filling in the empty spaces. Sew to the quilt using a whipstitch as before.

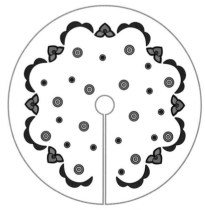

Appliquéd tree skirt

MANTEL SCARF

This is perfect for decorating your mantel, but if you don't have one, don't worry. It works equally well on a shelf or bookcase. The instructions are easily modified to fit the dimensions of your intended space.

FINISHED MANTEL SCARF: 36″ × 18½″

MATERIALS

Refer to Color Options (page 6) and Mantel Scarf patterns (pages 76 and 77).

COLORS AND QUANTITY OF WOOL FELT		
COLOR	PATTERN	AMOUNT NEEDED
Barnyard Red	20-A	5 squares 1¼″ × 1¼″
Butternut Squash	20-B	5 squares 2″ × 2″
Butternut Squash	20-C	4 squares 1¼″ × 1¼″
Fresh Linen	20-D	4 squares 1¾″ × 1¾″
Pea Soup	20-E	4 rectangles 2″ × 2½″
Tropical Wave	20-F	8 rectangles 2½″ × 3½″
Fresh Linen	20-G	3 squares 3¾″ × 3¾″
Tropical Wave	20-G	2 squares 3¾″ × 3¾″
Tropical Wave	20-H	3 squares 3″ × 3″
Pea Soup	20-H	2 squares 3″ × 3″
Pea Soup	20-I	3 rectangles 5¼″ × 6½″
Fresh Linen	20-I	2 rectangles 5¼″ × 6½″
Barnyard Red	20-J	10 rectangles 6″ × 7½″
Barnyard Red	Background*	1 rectangle 12″ × 36″

* Measure your mantel or the intended shelf before cutting the background piece. Cut the piece about ½″ wider than the shelf; for example, if your mantel is 8″, cut the background 8½″ × 36″. My shelf was 11½″ deep.

Other supplies:

■ Embroidery floss in assorted colors

■ Freezer paper

INSTRUCTIONS

Refer to Information for All Projects (page 9) for basic information on making and using templates and sewing.

1. Make the freezer-paper templates and cut the felt pieces.

2. Center a circle 20-A on a circle 20-B and sew together using a whipstitch.

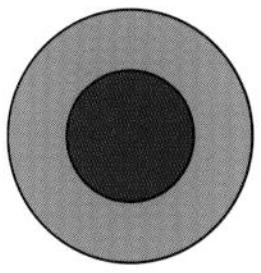

Make 5.

3. Center a circle 20-C on a circle 20-D and sew together using a whipstitch.

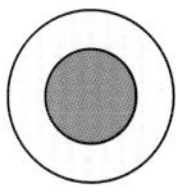

Make 4.

4. Place a shape 20-E on a shape 20-F as shown and sew together using a whipstitch.

Make 4.

5. Place a 20-C/D circle unit on a 20-E/F unit as shown and stitch together using a whipstitch around the edges of circle D. Place an appliquéd 20-C/D/E/F unit on a plain shape 20-F and stitch together along all the edges using a whipstitch.

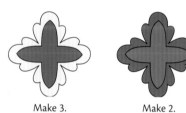

Make 4.

6. Center shape 20-H on shape 20-G and stitch together using a whipstitch.

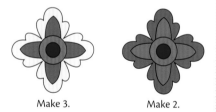

Make 3.   Make 2.

7. Center a 20-A/B circle unit on a 20-H/G unit and stitch together using a whipstitch around the edge of circle 20-B.

Make 3.   Make 2.

8. Center a 20-A/B/G/H unit on shape 20-I and stitch together using a whipstitch along the edge of shape 20-G.

Make 3.   Make 2.

9. Center a 20-A/B/G/H/I unit on a 20-J background and stitch together using a whipstitch.

Make 3.   Make 2.

10. Place an appliquéd 20-A/B/G/H/I/J unit on a plain 20-J background and stitch together along the edges using a whipstitch.

11. On a long edge of the background rectangle, press under ⅝" and machine stitch close to the fold.

12. Open out the folded-over felt and arrange the small and large units so that they butt up against the stitching and overlap the background felt by about ½". The stitching creates a ridge on the front that will rest on the edge of the mantel or shelf. Space the units evenly along the 36" background, trimming the background if necessary. (Stitching may cause the pieces to shrink up slightly.) Stitch the units in place along the top and ½" along each side.

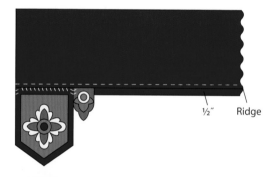

½"   Ridge

FINISHED TREE TOPPER: 8½" × 8½"

This project is like the cherry on top of the sundae! After decking the halls and trimming the tree, add this as the final touch to finish your holiday decor.

MATERIALS

Refer to Color Options (page 6) and Tree Topper patterns (page 78).

COLORS AND QUANTITY OF WOOL FELT		
COLOR	PATTERN	AMOUNT NEEDED
Butternut Squash	21-A	1 square 1¾" × 1¾"
Fresh Linen	21-B	1 square 3" × 3"
Tropical Wave	21-C	1 square 3¾" × 3¾"
Pea Soup	21-D	1 square 5" × 5"
Fresh Linen	21-E	1 square 7" × 7"
Barnyard Red	21-F	2 squares 9" × 9"
Barnyard Red	Rod pocket	1 rectangle 1" × 9"

Other supplies:
- Embroidery floss in assorted colors
- Low-loft cotton batting, 9" × 18" piece
- Freezer paper
- 36" wooden dowel, ¼" diameter
- Paint to match tree trunk
- Wire or twist ties

INSTRUCTIONS

Refer to Information for All Projects (page 9) for basic information on making and using templates and sewing.

1. Make the freezer-paper templates and cut the felt pieces.

- *To make freezer-paper templates for shapes 21-D and 21-E, fold 2 squares 7" × 7" of freezer paper in quarters with the dull side out. Trace the pattern onto the freezer paper as indicated on the pattern.*

- *To make a freezer-paper template for shape 21-F, fold a 9" × 9" square of freezer paper in quarters with the dull side out. Trace the pattern onto the freezer paper as indicated on the pattern.*

2. Center circle 21-A on star shape 21-B and sew together using a whipstitch.

3. Center unit 21-A/B on flower shape 21-C and sew together using a whipstitch around the edges of star shape 21-B. Add embroidery stitches as shown, using French knots, lazy daisy stitch, and running stitch.

4. Center shape 21-E on shape 21-F and sew together using a whipstitch.

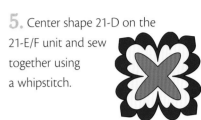

5. Center shape 21-D on the 21-E/F unit and sew together using a whipstitch.

6. Center unit 21-A/B/C on unit 21-D/E/F and sew together using a whipstitch around the edges of flower shape 21-C. Add French knots along the edge of shape 21-E.

7. Cut 2 pieces of cotton batting using the 21-F template and trim ¼" from all the edges. Place the appliquéd unit on the plain shape 21-F with the batting sandwiched in between and stitch together along the edges using a whipstitch.

8. Place the 1" × 9" piece of felt for the rod pocket on the back of shape 21-F, positioned vertically from the top to the bottom. Stitch the rod pocket to the back of the tree topper along both long sides and the top using a whipstitch. Take care not to stitch through to the front.

9. Cut the wooden dowel to the length needed for your tree and paint it. When it is dry, insert it into the pocket on the back of the tree topper. To attach the topper to your tree, slip the dowel down along the trunk from the top of the tree and hold it in place with wire or a few twist ties.

Appliqué Patterns

ORNAMENT COLLECTION

ORNAMENT BACKGROUNDS
(Ornaments, pages 12–29)

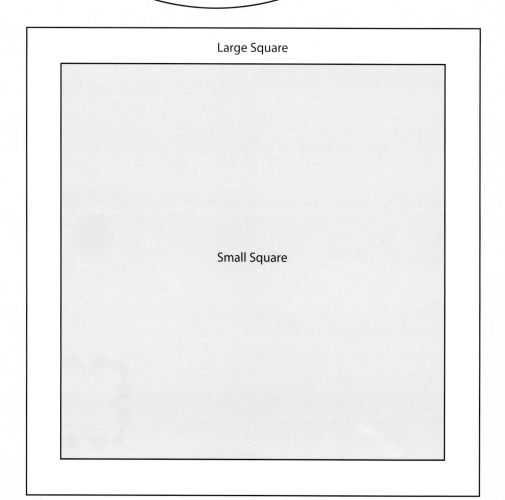

Large Circle

Small Circle

Large Square

Small Square

MERRY ORNAMENT

(Merry, page 12)

1-A Small
Cut 1.

1-A Large
Cut 1.

1-B Large
Cut 1.

1-B Small
Cut 1.

1-C Small
Cut 1.

1-C Large
Cut 1.

1-D Large
Cut 1.

1-E Large
Cut 1.

1-D Small
Cut 1.

1-E Small
Cut 1.

NOEL ORNAMENT

(Noel, page 14)

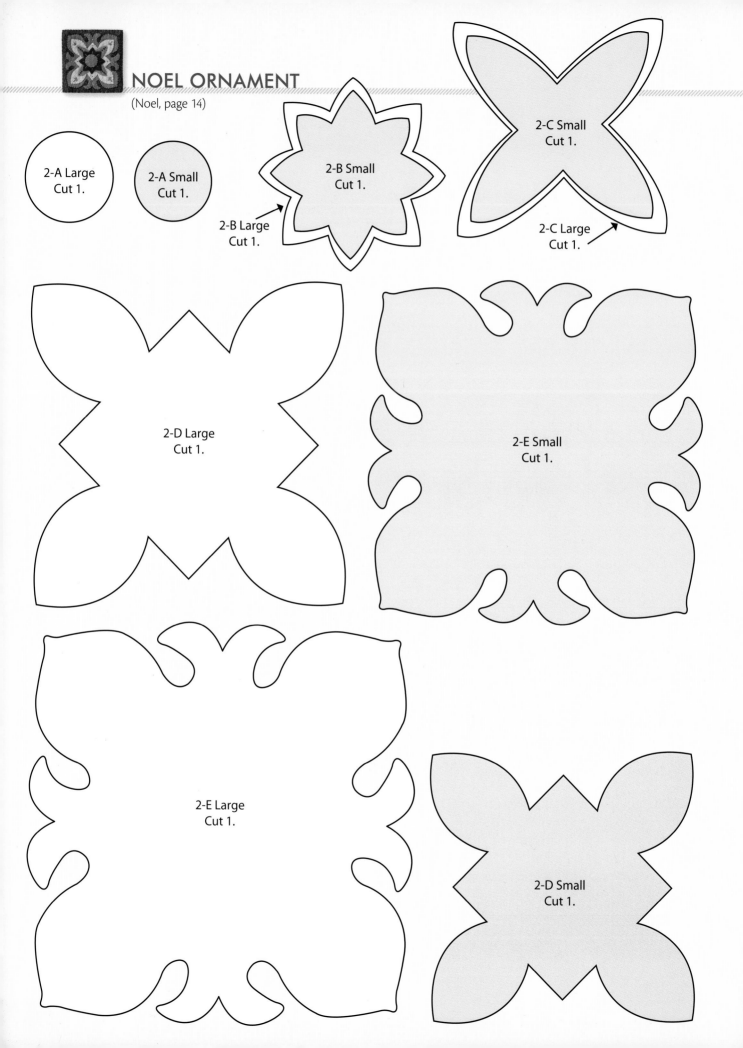

2-A Large
Cut 1.

2-A Small
Cut 1.

2-B Small
Cut 1.

2-B Large
Cut 1.

2-C Small
Cut 1.

2-C Large
Cut 1.

2-D Large
Cut 1.

2-E Small
Cut 1.

2-E Large
Cut 1.

2-D Small
Cut 1.

STARLIGHT ORNAMENT

(Starlight, page 16)

3-A Large
Cut 1.

3-B Large
Cut 1.

3-A Small
Cut 1.

3-B Small
Cut 1.

3-C Small
Cut 1.

3-C Large
Cut 1.

3-D Large
Cut 1.

3-E Large
Cut 1.

3-D Small
Cut 1.

3-E Small
Cut 1.

(Holly, page 18)

4-A Large
Cut 1.

4-A Small
Cut 1.

4-B Small
Cut 1.

4-B Large
Cut 1.

4-C Small
Cut 1.

4-C Large
Cut 1.

4-D Large
Cut 1.

4-D Small
Cut 1.

GLITTER ORNAMENT

(Glitter, page 20)

5-A Large
Cut 1.

5-A Small
Cut 1.

5-C Small
Cut 1.

5-C Large
Cut 1.

5-B Large
Cut 1.

5-B Small
Cut 1.

5-D Small
Cut 1.

5-D Large
Cut 1.

JOLLY ORNAMENT

(Jolly, page 22)

6-A Small
Cut 1.

6-B Small
Cut 1.

6-A Large
Cut 1.

6-B Large
Cut 1.

6-C Small
Cut 4.

6-C Large
Cut 4.

6-D Large
Cut 1.

6-E Small
Cut 1.

6-E Large
Cut 1.

6-D Small
Cut 1.

JOY ORNAMENT

(Joy, page 24)

7-A Large
Cut 1.

7-A Small
Cut 1.

7-B Small
Cut 1.

7-B Large
Cut 1.

7-C Small
Cut 1.

7-C Large
Cut 1.

7-D Large
Cut 1.

7-D Small
Cut 1.

FLURRY ORNAMENT

(Flurry, page 26)

8-A Small
Cut 1.

8-B Small
Cut 1.

8-A Large
Cut 1.

8-B Large
Cut 1.

8-D Large
Cut 1.

8-C Small
Cut 1.

8-C Large
Cut 1.

8-D Small
Cut 1.

8-E Small
Cut 1.

8-E Large
Cut 1.

JINGLE ORNAMENT

(Jingle, page 28)

9-A Large
Cut 1.

9-B Large
Cut 1.

9-A Small
Cut 1.

9-B Small
Cut 1.

9-C Large
Cut 1.

9-C Small
Cut 1.

9-D Large
Cut 1.

9-D Small
Cut 1.

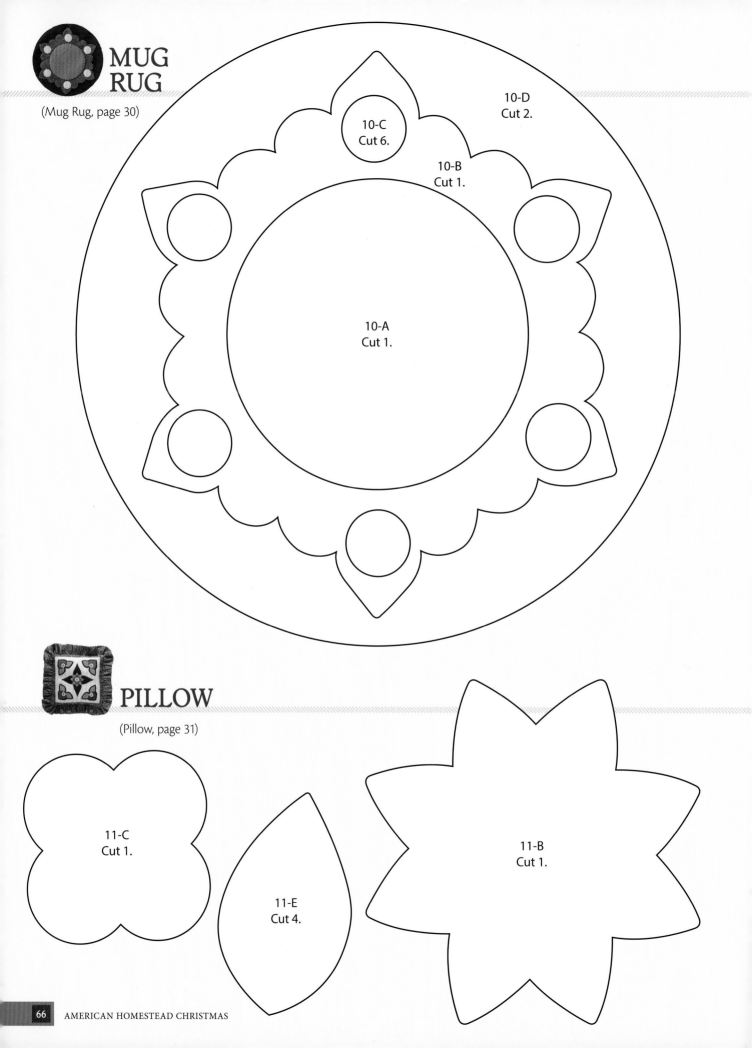

MUG RUG

(Mug Rug, page 30)

10-C
Cut 6.

10-D
Cut 2.

10-B
Cut 1.

10-A
Cut 1.

PILLOW

(Pillow, page 31)

11-C
Cut 1.

11-E
Cut 4.

11-B
Cut 1.

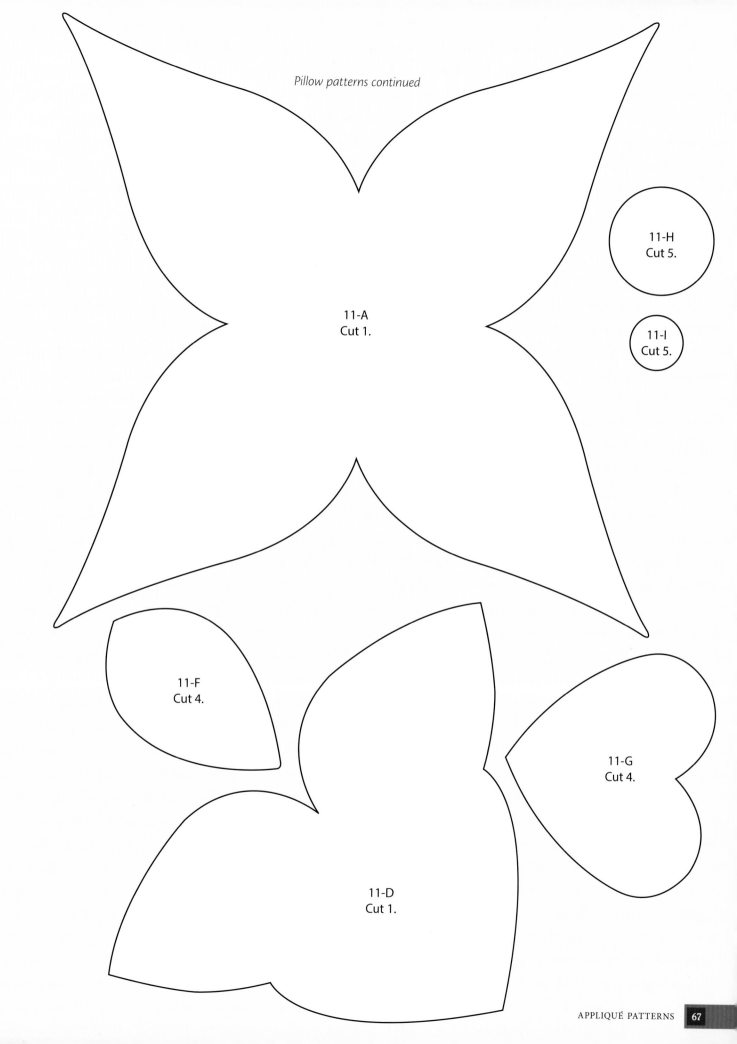

Pillow patterns continued

11-H
Cut 5.

11-I
Cut 5.

11-A
Cut 1.

11-F
Cut 4.

11-G
Cut 4.

11-D
Cut 1.

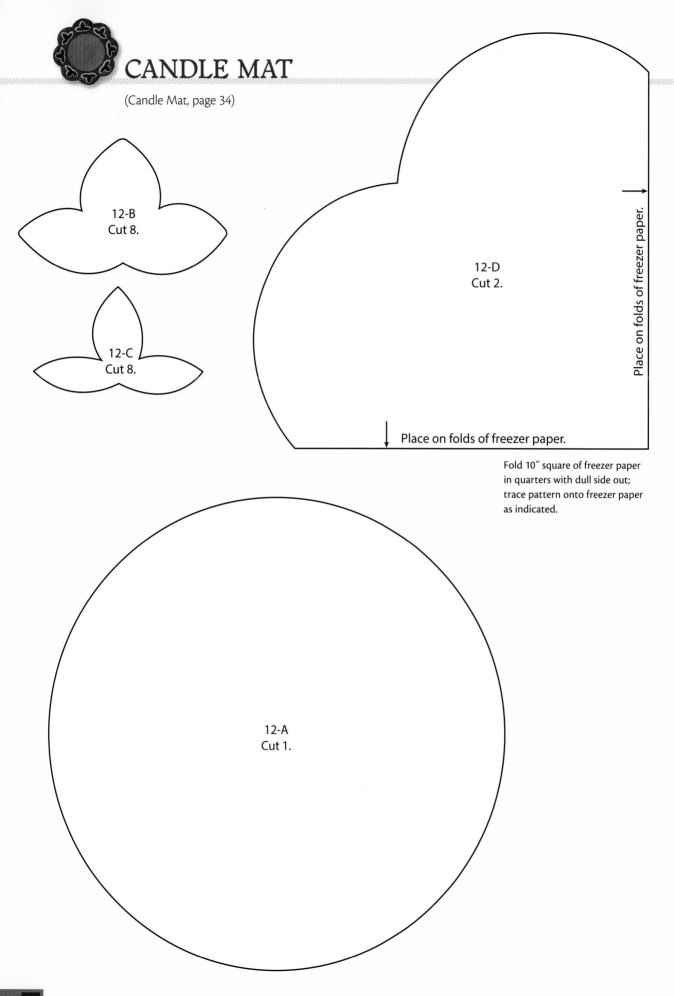

CANDLE MAT

(Candle Mat, page 34)

12-B
Cut 8.

12-C
Cut 8.

12-D
Cut 2.

Place on folds of freezer paper.

Place on folds of freezer paper.

Fold 10″ square of freezer paper
in quarters with dull side out;
trace pattern onto freezer paper
as indicated.

12-A
Cut 1.

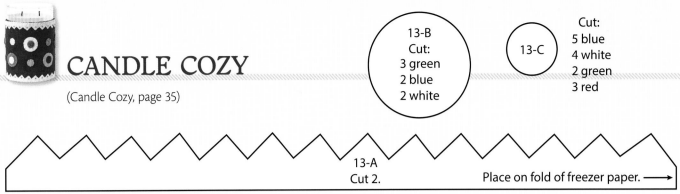

CANDLE COZY

(Candle Cozy, page 35)

13-B
Cut:
3 green
2 blue
2 white

13-C

Cut:
5 blue
4 white
2 green
3 red

13-A
Cut 2.

Place on fold of freezer paper. →

Fold 1½" × 15" piece of freezer paper in half with dull side out;
trace pattern onto freezer paper as indicated.

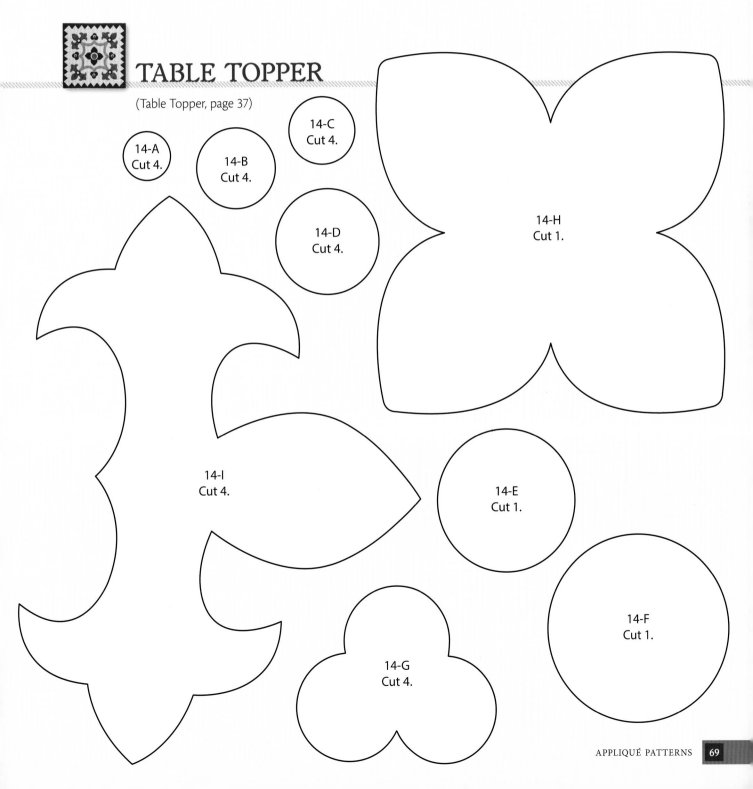

TABLE TOPPER

(Table Topper, page 37)

14-A
Cut 4.

14-B
Cut 4.

14-C
Cut 4.

14-D
Cut 4.

14-H
Cut 1.

14-I
Cut 4.

14-E
Cut 1.

14-F
Cut 1.

14-G
Cut 4.

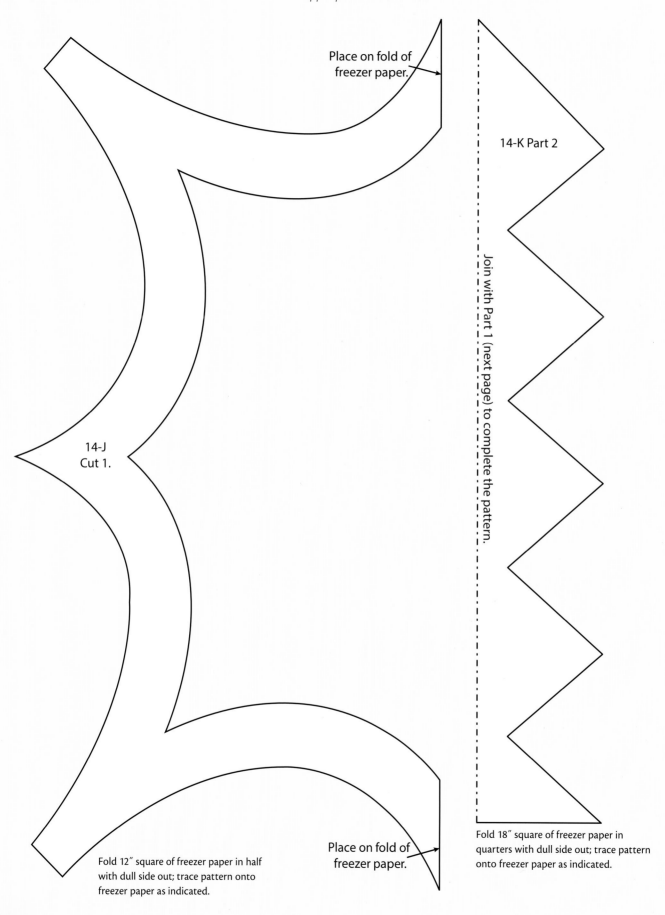

Place on fold of
freezer paper.

14-K Part 2

Join with Part 1 (next page) to complete the pattern.

14-J
Cut 1.

Place on fold of
freezer paper.

Fold 12" square of freezer paper in half
with dull side out; trace pattern onto
freezer paper as indicated.

Fold 18" square of freezer paper in
quarters with dull side out; trace pattern
onto freezer paper as indicated.

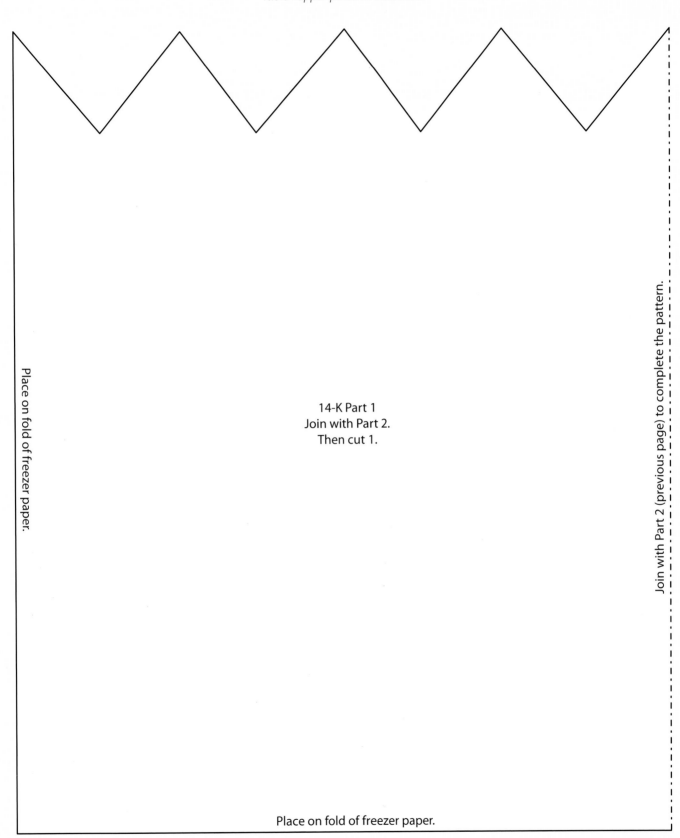

Place on fold of freezer paper.

14-K Part 1
Join with Part 2.
Then cut 1.

Join with Part 2 (previous page) to complete the pattern.

Place on fold of freezer paper.

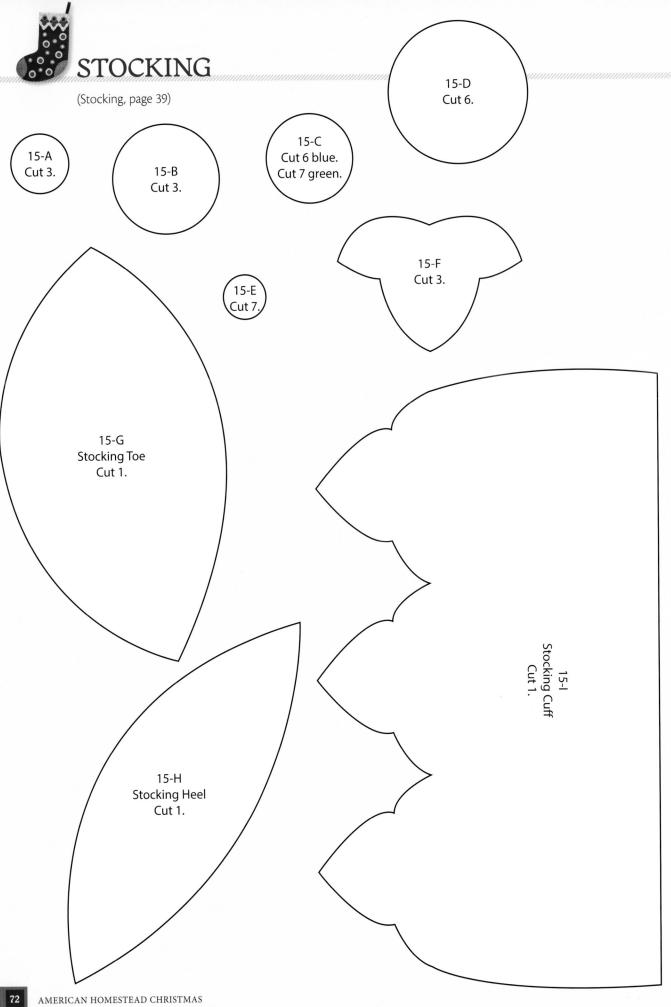

STOCKING

(Stocking, page 39)

15-A
Cut 3.

15-B
Cut 3.

15-C
Cut 6 blue.
Cut 7 green.

15-D
Cut 6.

15-E
Cut 7.

15-F
Cut 3.

15-G
Stocking Toe
Cut 1.

15-H
Stocking Heel
Cut 1.

15-I
Stocking Cuff
Cut 1.

15-J
Stocking Top

Join with Stocking Bottom (page 74) to complete the pattern.

15-J
Stocking Toe

Join with Stocking Bottom (page 74) to complete the pattern.

Join with Stocking Toe (page 73) to complete the pattern.

15-J
Stocking Bottom
Join Stocking Top, Bottom, and Toe.
Then cut 2.

Join with Stocking Top (page 73) to complete the pattern.

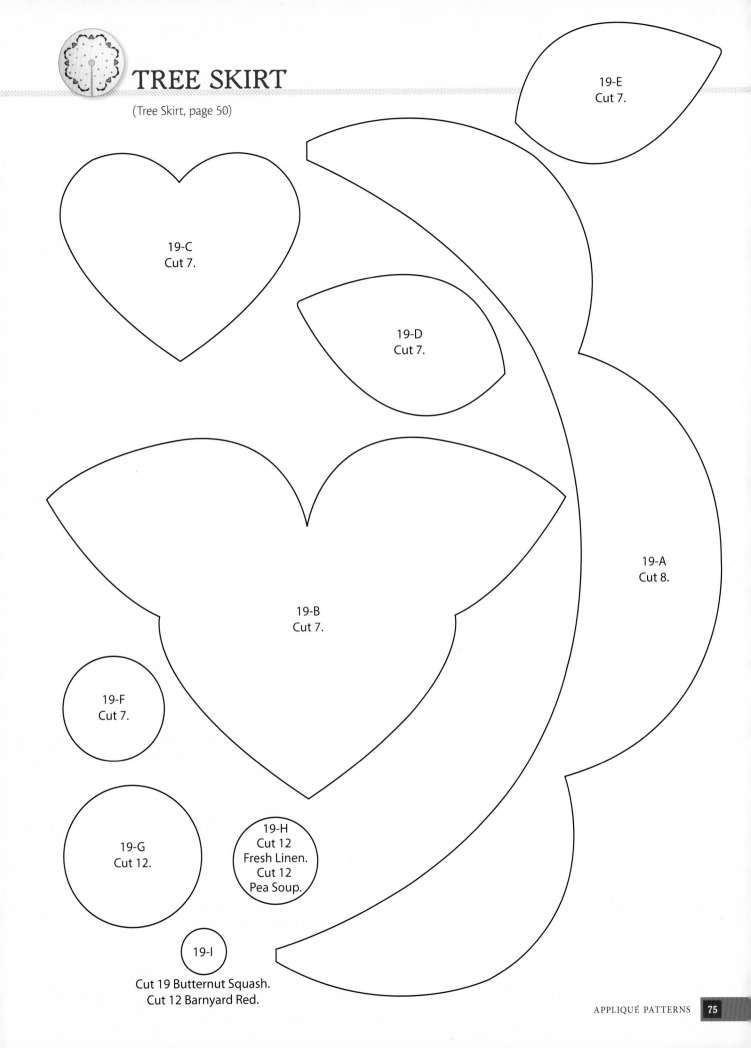

TREE SKIRT

(Tree Skirt, page 50)

19-E
Cut 7.

19-C
Cut 7.

19-D
Cut 7.

19-A
Cut 8.

19-B
Cut 7.

19-F
Cut 7.

19-G
Cut 12.

19-H
Cut 12
Fresh Linen.
Cut 12
Pea Soup.

19-I

Cut 19 Butternut Squash.
Cut 12 Barnyard Red.

MANTEL SCARF

(Mantel Scarf, page 53)

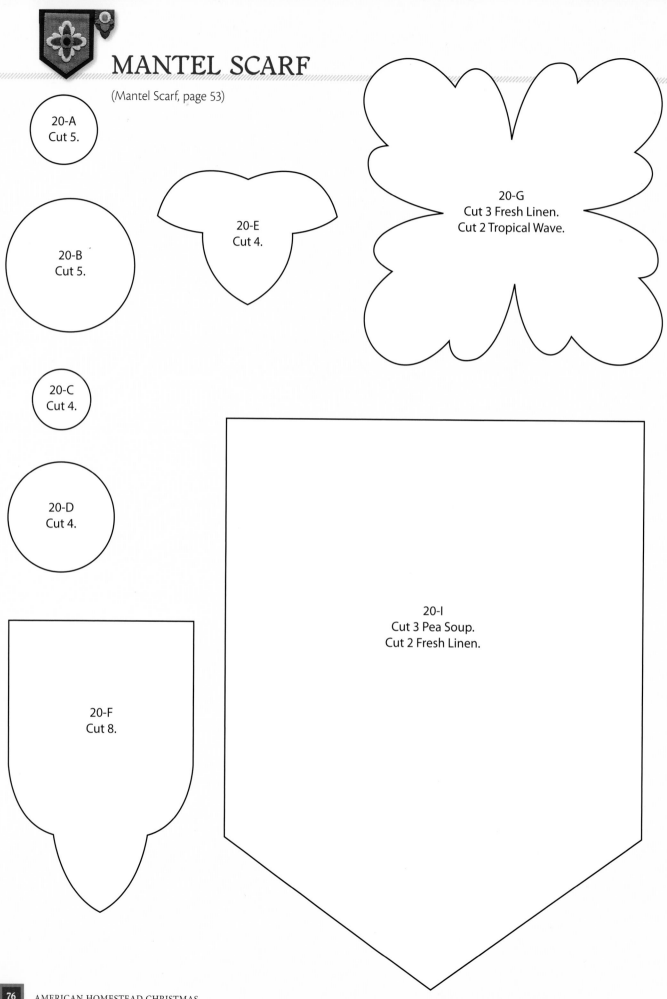

20-A
Cut 5.

20-B
Cut 5.

20-E
Cut 4.

20-G
Cut 3 Fresh Linen.
Cut 2 Tropical Wave.

20-C
Cut 4.

20-D
Cut 4.

20-I
Cut 3 Pea Soup.
Cut 2 Fresh Linen.

20-F
Cut 8.

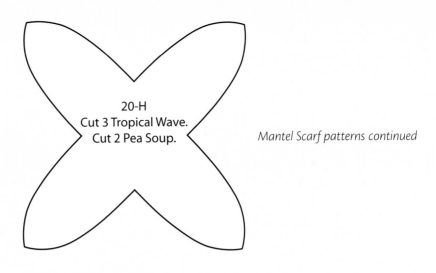

20-H
Cut 3 Tropical Wave.
Cut 2 Pea Soup.

Mantel Scarf patterns continued

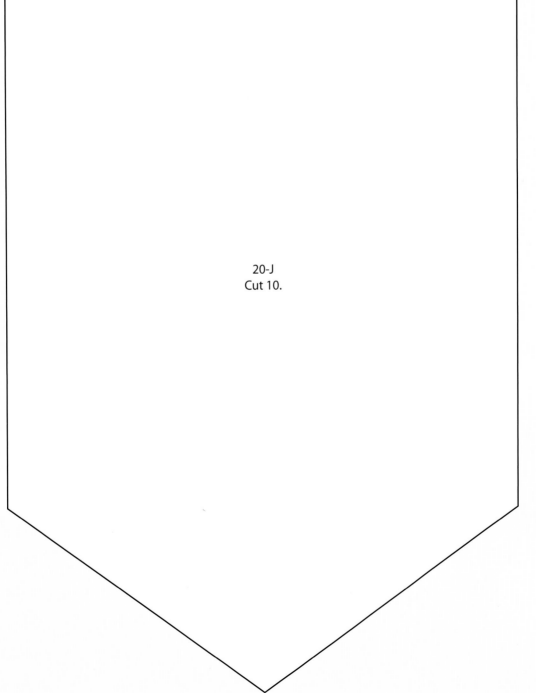

20-J
Cut 10.

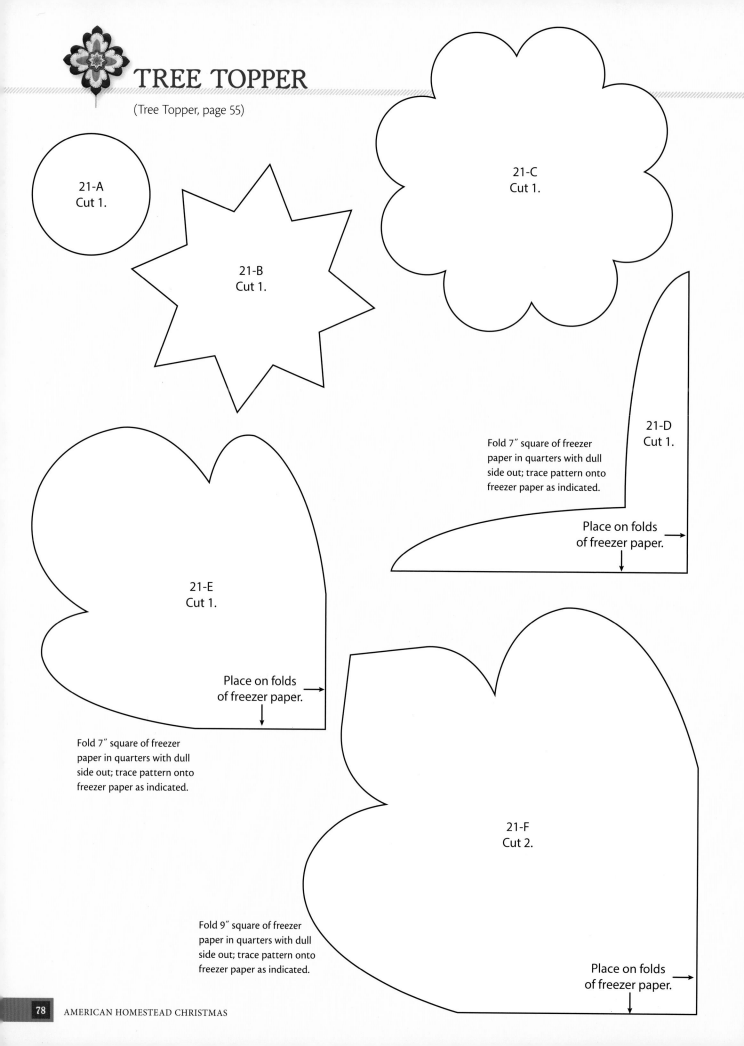

TREE TOPPER

(Tree Topper, page 55)

21-A
Cut 1.

21-B
Cut 1.

21-C
Cut 1.

21-D
Cut 1.

Fold 7″ square of freezer paper in quarters with dull side out; trace pattern onto freezer paper as indicated.

Place on folds of freezer paper.

21-E
Cut 1.

Place on folds of freezer paper.

Fold 7″ square of freezer paper in quarters with dull side out; trace pattern onto freezer paper as indicated.

21-F
Cut 2.

Fold 9″ square of freezer paper in quarters with dull side out; trace pattern onto freezer paper as indicated.

Place on folds of freezer paper.

ABOUT THE AUTHOR

Ellen Murphy says she was born with a crayon in her hand. She has loved art and design her entire life. Since she was a teenager, she has loved quilting and has always enjoyed manipulating fabric—whether for garment construction or craft pursuits. Ellen has a degree in fine art and a strong love of color. Working in graphic design and as a quilting/craft teacher taught her to create patterns that are easy to understand.

Ellen loves to travel, and that love has taken her around the world. She brings the inspiration she receives from her journeys to her designs. Ellen is the owner and designer of American Homestead, a craft pattern design company.

See what Ellen is up to at:

- americanhomesteaddesign.com

Or on her blogs:

- americanhomestead.blogspot.com
- chock-a-blockquiltblocks.blogspot.com
- homesteadtravels.blogspot.com

Also by Ellen Murphy:

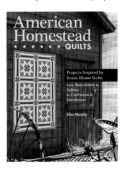

RESOURCES

The materials used for the projects in this book are available at your local quilt, craft, or hobby store, or from the sources listed.

FELT

- **National Nonwovens**
  commonwealthfelt.com

HOT FIX RHINESTONES AND CRYSTALS

- Dollar Trims and Beads
  dollartrimsandbeads.com
  (*or* squareup.com/market/
  dollar-trims-and-beads)

QUILTMAKING BASICS

- *All-in-One Quilter's Reference Tool, Updated Second Edition* by Harriet Hargrave, Sharyn Craig, Alex Anderson, and Liz Aneloski

- *The Practical Guide to Patchwork* by Elizabeth Hartman

- C&T Publishing
  ctpub.com

Great Titles and Products

from C&T PUBLISHING and stashBOOKS®

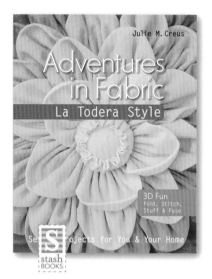

Available at your local retailer or **ctpub.com** *or* **800-284-1114**

For a list of other fine books from C&T Publishing, visit our website to view our catalog online.

C&T PUBLISHING, INC.

P.O. Box 1456
Lafayette, CA 94549
800-284-1114

Email: ctinfo@ctpub.com
Website: ctpub.com

Tips and techniques can be found at ctpub.com/quilting-sewing-tips.

For quilting supplies:

COTTON PATCH

1025 Brown Ave.
Lafayette, CA 94549
Store: 925-284-1177
Mail order: 925-283-7883

Email: CottonPa@aol.com
Website: quiltusa.com

Note: Fabrics shown may not be currently available, as fabric manufacturers keep most fabrics in print for only a short time.